Becoming More Like Jesus

Also by Bert Ghezzi

Transforming Problems
The Angry Christian
Facing Your Feelings
Getting Free
Emotions as Resources (with Mark Kinzer)
Build With the Lord

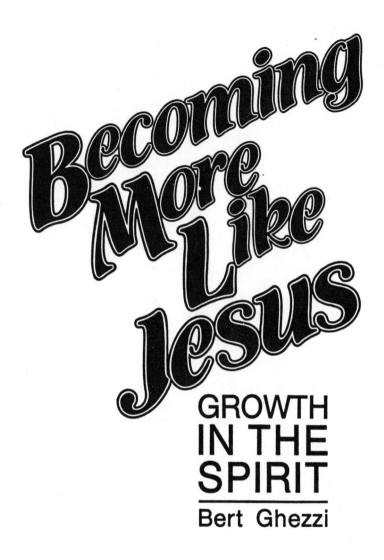

GROWTH
IN THE
SPIRIT

Bert Ghezzi

Our Sunday Visitor Publishing Division
Our Sunday Visitor, Inc.
Huntington, Indiana 46750

ACKNOWLEDGMENTS: Scripture texts contained in this work are quoted verbatim or paraphrased from the *Jerusalem Bible* (JB) and from the *Revised Standard Version, Catholic Edition* (RSV). The JB is © 1966 by Darton, Longman & Todd, Ltd., and Doubleday & Company, Inc., all rights reserved. The RSV is © 1965 and 1966 by the Division of Christian Education of the National Council of the Churches of Christ in the U.S.A., all rights reserved. Other sources from which material has been excerpted or has served as the basis for portions of this work are cited in the chapter notes. The author is grateful to the copyright holders for the use of their materials. If any copyrighted materials have been inadvertently used in this book without proper credit being given, please notify Our Sunday Visitor in writing so that future printings of this work may be corrected accordingly.

Our Sunday Visitor Publishing Division
Our Sunday Visitor, Inc.
200 Noll Plaza
Huntington, Indiana 46750

International Standard Book Number: 0-87973-518-X
Library of Congress Catalog Card Number: 86-63424

Cover design by James E. McIlrath

PRINTED IN THE UNITED STATES OF AMERICA

518

For Mary Lou ————————————————

Contents

PART ONE

The Fruit
of the
Spirit

Replicas of God

1

In *The Screwtape Letters*, C.S. Lewis imagines correspondence between Screwtape, a master devil, and his nephew Wormwood, a junior devil in training. Screwtape is coaching Wormwood in the art of seducing souls and is educating him in the psychology of temptation. At one point, he compares the ultimate purpose of Satan, his Father below, with that of God, his Enemy above.

"To us a human is primarily food," Screwtape explains. "Our aim is the absorption of its will into ours." Disgusting as it is to Screwtape, his Enemy loves humans and has unbelievably good plans for them. "One must face the fact," writes the senior devil, "that all the talk about His love for men is not mere propaganda, but an appalling truth. He really *does* want to fill the universe with a lot of loathsome little replicas of Himself — creatures whose life, on its miniature scale, will be qualitatively like His own, not because He has absorbed them but because their wills freely conform to His. We want cattle who can finally become food; He wants servants who can finally become sons [and daughters]."[1]

In a nutshell this is the purpose of God in creating men and women. He wants millions of sons and daughters, crafted in his own image and likeness, who will en-

9

joy, care for, and rule his creation with him (Genesis 1:26-28). This also sums up God's reason for sending his only Son to become one of us. Jesus founded the Church, in which all who believe in him can have a relationship with God as his sons and daughters (Galatians 3:26).

If you are like me, you may find it easy to reject the idea that we are replicas of God, contending that it is a nice theory but does not seem to fit the reality we know. There is too much evidence to the contrary. Our weaknesses, faults, and sins tell us convincingly that we are not very much like God.

These facts, however, are not contradictory. We are made in God's likeness, but we are flawed. Sin clouds his image in us so that we must be continually renewed in it. Paul put it this way in his Letter to the Colossians (3:8-10 / RSV): "But now put them all away: anger, wrath, malice, slander, and foul talk from your mouth. Do not lie to one another, seeing that you have put off the old nature with its practices and have put on *the new nature, which is being renewed in knowledge after the image of its creator.*" (Emphasis mine.)

The Christians at Colossae were renewed in God's image, just as we are. Yet sometimes they got violently angry, slandered someone, or lied, just as we do. At these moments they did not resemble God very much. However, they had traded their old sinful nature for a new nature in Christ, just as we have.

Notice that Paul says it is our new nature in Christ — not the deformed old man in us — that is constantly being renewed in God's image. No matter how messy we may look, no matter how distorted his likeness in us may occasionally become, we really are sons and daughters of God. We are new creations that are free to serve God or to offend him. That terrible freedom is part of what it means to be his replicas. Most exciting is the possibility that we can become more like him.

PUTTING ON JESUS CHRIST

If we are to be recognized as God's sons and daughters, we must show our relationship to him by behaving as he would. This is not easy, as God has been known to behave in ways we find repulsive and hard to imitate. Jesus, for example, ordered us to love our enemies and to pray for our persecutors "so that you may be sons [and daughters] of your Father who is in heaven; for he makes his sun rise on the evil and on the good, and sends rain on the just and on the unjust" (Matthew 5:44-45 / RSV). And from his cross Jesus gave us the supreme example of love and forgiveness.

After telling the Colossians that they were being renewed in God's image, Paul instructed them in attributes that would make them more like Christ: "Put on then . . . compassion, kindness, lowliness, meekness, and patience, forbearing one another and, if one has a complaint against another, forgiving each other; . . . And above all these put on love, which binds everything together in perfect harmony" (3:12-14 / RSV).

Paul's analogy is to put on character traits even as we might put on clothes. Sons and daughters of God must dress the part. There is a story told of a young pauper that illustrates the point. A boy in his late teens lived as a beggar in a town on the frontier of a great kingdom. He was very rough cut, illiterate, and uncouth. One day the king visited the town and paraded

11

down the main street. The youth elbowed his way through the crowd to catch a glimpse of the monarch and his entourage.

A high official of the court identified the youth as the long-lost son of the king. He had the royal guards bring the lad to the monarch, who also recognized him as his son and heir. The king ordered that the youth be attended by servants, bathed, and dressed in royal robes. He arranged for his son's education and training so that the young man could conduct himself with appropriate princely bearing.

That's the way it is with God and us. We are his sons and daughters. He has arranged for us to be cleansed and dressed so that our bearing reflects our relationship to him. The clothes we put on are qualities that declare our likeness to God. For example, the list in Colossians 3 specifies compassion, kindness, lowliness, meekness, patience, forbearance, and love. We call such traits the fruit, or fruits, of the Holy Spirit. (I have decided to use "fruit" instead of "fruits," except in random cases involving quoted matter.)

THE FRUIT OF THE HOLY SPIRIT

More familiar is the list found in Galatians 5:22-23 / RSV; Paul says, "The fruit of the Spirit is love, joy, peace, patience, kindness, goodness, faithfulness, gentleness, self-control." When we do loving things, when we are joyful in tough circumstances, when we are peacemakers, when we are patient with difficult people, when we set aside meanness so as to be kind, when we are generous with our limited resources, when we can be relied on to keep our word, when we control ourselves — then our behavior radiates the image of God.

Jesus taught plainly about the importance of spiritual fruit, warning us in Matthew 7:15-20 / JB: "Beware of false prophets who come to you disguised as sheep but underneath are ravenous wolves. You will be able to tell them by their fruits. Can people pick grapes from thorns, or figs from thistles? In the same way, a sound tree produces good fruit but a rotten tree bad fruit. A sound tree cannot bear bad fruit, nor a rotten tree bear good fruit. Any tree that does not produce good fruit is cut down and thrown on the fire. I repeat, you will be able to tell them by their fruits."

Our Lord places a higher priority on spiritual fruit than he does on dramatic spiritual phenomena. Prophecy, exorcism, and miracles may attract our attention, but the Lord rivets his attention on love, joy, peace, and the like.

When we finally come into the heavenly court and stand before God, he will not recognize us by our accomplishments, which will add up to very little, no matter how important they seem to us; he will know us instead by our resemblance to Jesus. He will be looking to see if we bear Jesus' image and if we produced the fruit of the Holy Spirit. He will scrutinize our lives, looking for qualities like patience and generosity. Was this man kind to his wife? Was he gentle with his children? Was this woman a woman of peace? Did she forgive people who hurt her? These questions are the kind that the just Judge will ask about us.

One miracle of the Christian life is that we who realize we are so bad, can really bear good fruit. When we are baptized into Christ, he transforms us radically so that we can grow to be more like him every day. The fruit of the Spirit are attributes that sharpen the divine image in us and bring it back into focus. They change us into more exact replicas of God.

More Than Feelings 2

Many Christians today have lost interest in the fruit of the Holy Spirit. They would like to have them, but they think they have tried them and found them wanting. Their introduction to the fruit of the Spirit offered dynamic new qualities, but when they received the fruit they were disappointed. Like some glittering gizmos offered on late-night TV, the fruit of the Spirit seemed to fall short of what the promotion promised.

That was my experience, and it may also have been yours. I learned about the fruit of the Spirit as preparation for the sacrament of confirmation, which in the 1950s most Catholic children received at about age thirteen. We spent a whole school year getting ready to be filled with the power of the Holy Spirit.

Anticipation ran high as the big day drew nearer. Girls got new pastel-colored dresses; boys got navy-blue trousers, white dress shirts, and red silk ties. Parties were planned. We had rehearsals every day the week before the bishop would visit our church for the big event. I was excited because I expected the gifts and fruit of the Spirit to make a dramatic difference in my life.

The wonderful day came at last. The ceremonies were splendid. The bishop told us that the Holy Spirit would make us soldiers of Christ, a truth that had been drummed into us all year. He anointed each of us with oil and prayed that we would receive the Holy Spirit.

I regarded the event as a big letdown. After confirmation, I didn't feel any different. I thought that having love, joy, and peace would mean that I would feel more loving, more joyful, and more peaceful. I was mistaken. Not only did nothing seem to happen, but I also got depressed over it. All the confusion and fears of puberty were beginning to wallop me. If I had become a soldier of Christ, I felt like a pretty weak one.

In defense of my teachers, I have to say that I agree that building anticipation is a sound way to introduce people to life in the Holy Spirit. Our expectancy expresses our faith that God is going to do something for us. The Lord is a God who acts, and faith is our way of receiving from him.

ACTIVE AND EXTERNAL

Many years later I discovered that I had been mistaken about the fruit of the Spirit. I had thought they were something they were not. I had expected less of them than they are, for I learned that they are better, more valuable, and more significant than mere feelings.

My enlightening occurred during a talk on the subject by a friend of mine. He startled me by asserting that the fruit of the Spirit were not mainly feelings or internal states. He said they were patterns of behavior or character traits. His point was that feelings were internal reactions, whereas the fruit of the Spirit were chiefly active and external. That was news to me.

My friend based his assertion on the context of

Galatians 5. Paul, by way of comparison to the fruit of the Spirit, presents there a list of the works of the flesh, including fornication, impurity, licentiousness, idolatry, sorcery, enmity, strife, jealousy, anger, selfishness, dissension, party spirit, envy, drunkenness, and carousing (Galatians 5:19-21). These "fruit of the flesh" are mainly activities people do outside themselves, often involving others. Internal states such as jealousy or enmity become full blown when they drive us to hurt someone. While people who fornicate, fight, or carouse may do it with feeling, emotion is only a part and not always even a major part of the action.

In this context, the fruit of the Spirit must be understood the same way. Love, for example, does not simply mean feeling attracted to someone or feeling warmly toward another. It also means expressing affection and doing things loved ones will appreciate, such as unexpectedly undertaking one of their chores, avoiding behavior that irks them, or listening carefully when they are speaking. Joy too refers both to feeling happy and to the activities that express rejoicing, such as throwing a party, celebrating by going out with friends, dancing, singing, and so on. All of these are external things that may be done with more or less feeling. And peace, while it does not exclude a sense of restfulness and well-being, also denotes the unity we get by working hard at loving other people.

POWERFUL RESOURCES

The context of Galatians 5 also helps us to appreciate the real value of the fruit of the Spirit. Propelled by self-indulgence, we hurt one another. Paul's

17

list of the ways self-indulgence warps and wounds relationships — all the way from fornication down to drunken orgies — is a catalog of potent destructiveness. If anything can overcome such forces as these, it will have to have clout.

We may imagine that the fruit of the Spirit are nice, positive qualities that God deposits in us. We may even think of them as somewhat passive virtues nestled in among our nastier qualities, where they may be jostled, bruised, and beaten down. These are common misconceptions.

In reality, the fruit of the Spirit are not namby-pamby graces that cower in the presence of such menaces as lust, envy, or hatred. Faced with the works of the flesh, the fruit of the Spirit do not go for coexistence. They are after conquest. Paul says that all who belong to Christ have crucified the self with all of its passions and desires (Galatians 5:24). So the fruit of the Spirit are not a polite veneer of niceness that conceals our badness and gives the false impression that we are like Christ. They are strong, aggressive resources that defang our evil tendencies. When they've done their work, we really are like Jesus from the inside out.

PAUL VERSUS HARRY

When my son Paul, who is now twenty years old, attended preschool, he got off to a rocky start with Harry, who was a loner, bullheaded, and picked on the girls. My wife, Mary Lou, and I explained to Paul that Harry's home life had been tough, his dad having left the family when Harry was an infant. We suggested to Paul that instead of grinding Harry's nose on the pavement, which Paul had done once or twice, he reach out to Harry and make him his friend.

"But I *hate* Harry," objected Paul, stating his feelings exactly.

"Treat him kindly anyway," urged his mother. "Invite him to play a game with you now and then."

Paul complied. He made some friendly overtures to Harry. After a few weeks, Paul and Harry had become buddies. Paul even campaigned for us to apply to become foster parents for Harry.

Love and the other fruit of the Spirit are like that. They are behavior patterns that may involve feelings but which cannot be reduced to them. I said above that the fruit of the Spirit are better, more valuable, and more significant than mere feelings. What I had in mind was their ability to harness the power of our emotions for good, as they did in the case of Paul versus Harry.

The Character Traits of Jesus

The fruit of the Spirit are not empty terms we can fill as we like. If that were the case, they would be meaningless, since every Christian would have his or her own definitions. Love, for example, would have little substance, since to some it would mean romance, to others friendship, and to still others commitment.

Even the lists of the fruit of the Spirit we find in Scripture — for example, Galatians 5:22 or Colossians 3:12-15 — don't give us a clear picture of what to expect from them. In order to understand and obtain these qualities, we must be able to find out what the Lord intends them to be.

God has shown us what he means by the fruit of the Spirit. He gave us Jesus, his Son, as an example of these qualities so that their meaning would be unmistakably plain.

The fruit of the Spirit are produced in people when their actions are inspired and directed by the Holy Spirit, and when they obey the Father as exactly as possible. No one has ever been more perfectly guided by the Holy Spirit than Jesus. No one has ever obeyed the Father more perfectly than he did. So, Jesus is a flawless example of the fruit of the Spirit for us to follow.

The fruit of the Spirit are the character traits of Jesus. Scriptural lists of them are inventories of the Lord's personality. In his responses to people and events, we can see how we are to live. If we want to become more like Jesus, we should reflect on his character. What was Jesus like? How did he treat this person? How did he handle himself in that situation? We can learn what the fruit of the Spirit are by observing Jesus in action.

Let's look, for example, at three sequences in the life of Jesus, identifying the fruit of the Spirit in his conduct. The stories — the wedding at Cana, the miracle of the loaves, and the crucifixion — are familiar, but we may never have considered them from this perspective.

√ *The wedding at Cana* (John 2:1-12). How did Jesus respond when his mother told him that the family had run out of wine? At first he reminded Mary that the moment for initiating the course of events that would inevitably take him to the cross had not yet come. However, Mary knew his character. She enlisted the servants' help, as she was sure that Jesus would not refuse her.

What qualities do we see in Jesus here? He showed his love for Mary by responding kindly to her request. He was compassionate to the young couple, preventing their embarrassment. He even enhanced their reputation by providing a better wine than they had already served.

Most of all, Jesus acted humbly. He knew the timetable was not exactly right for signs and wonders that would stir interest in him. He could have refused to act, insisting that he had more important priorities. Instead, he changed his course out of deference to Mary. He put

21

the interests of his mother and the wedding couple ahead of his own interests, knowing that by doing so he would be carrying forward God's plans.

√ *The miracle of the loaves* (Matthew 14:13-21). Jesus' behavior here is all the more fascinating if we recall that he has just been told that John the Baptist has been beheaded. Touched by grief, he tried to be alone with his disciples. He may also have felt a twinge of fear, since the swirl of events leading to his own death were picking up in tempo.

However, the crowd would not let him be alone. At this point most of us would have reached the limits of our generosity, and we would have dismissed the crowds.

"Don't they realize I have needs too?" we might have complained. But not Jesus. He took pity on them, healed their sick, and seized the opportunity to feed them miraculously. The love of Jesus was never selfish. He sought no mercy for himself, but always showed mercy.

√ *The crucifixion* (Luke 22:14-23, 46). In the last fifteen hours of his life, including the three hours he hung dying on the cross, Jesus' character shone radiantly. Consider the following examples of fruit of the Spirit he manifested then:

Patience. Jesus dealt patiently with the disciples who argued about who among them was the greatest (Luke 22:25-27). He was patient with Peter, James, and John, who were unable to stay awake to pray (Matthew 26:42-45).

Self-control. Jesus experienced a swarm of strong emotions: frustration at apparent failures; anger at the blindness of his opponents; fear of death (Mark 14:33-34); rejection and betrayal by close friends; the shame and dishonor of the cross. Yet he walked through the terrible series of events in control of himself and of the situation.

Endurance. Jesus was scourged, mocked and spat upon, crowned with thorns, kept up all night, forced to carry his cross, and crucified. He accepted the pain of this torture without complaint.

Mercy. Jesus looked down from the cross, his body racked with pain, and asked his Father to forgive the men who had just crucified him (Luke 23:34).

Kindness. He promised the good thief he would meet him in paradise that very day (Luke 23:43).

Goodness. When Jesus was just about dead, he was still looking out for others. He asked a disciple to take care of Mary, his mother, only moments before he died (John 19:26-27).

Humility. Jesus, the God-man, humbly yielded to a shameful death on the cross (Philippians 2:8).

Love. Jesus' whole life was one great act of love that climaxed in his complete gift of self in the crucifixion.

Seeing the character of Jesus is seeing how God wants us to be. The Lord wants us to become more like Christ, which means that we must be marked by his distinctive qualities. Acquiring these traits, then, is very important to us.

GETTING THE PICTURE

On one occasion my daughter Mary, aged three, saw me sitting amid wheels, pedals, handlebars, tools, and instructions, and she asked: "What are you doing, Daddy?"

"This is going to be a bike, Mary, for you."

"For me?" she squealed with glee.

"Yes, for you. See this picture? That's what your bike will be like when I'm done," I said, adding under my breath, "If I can figure out these directions."

Showing Mary the picture of the bike helped her. She could anticipate that something exciting was about to happen to her. She ran off to tell her mother, brothers, and sisters. She returned all too soon to bug me to get it finished quicker. The picture also helped me assemble the bike correctly. Well, almost.

Having a picture of the end product we're aiming for is always helpful. For example, a boy from South America who has never seen an igloo could probably build a rough approximation, if he were given materials, descriptions, and plans. He would do a lot better, however, if he were shown a picture or even a real igloo. Seeing an igloo in advance would orient everything he had to do to construct it.

This principle applies to many areas of life, including our spiritual growth. Scripture tells us that we are being renewed in the image of God, and that the Holy Spirit produces traits that will make us Christ-like. It's natural for us to wonder what we're supposed to be like once we're transformed in Christ. While we're in the process of transformation, it would be helpful to have some picture of what the end product is supposed to be like. Is there some way to know in advance what I will be like when I have the fruit of the Spirit? If I had a model of Christian love, for example, it could orient all my behavior during my spiritual growth.

In reality, we do have models for Christian growth.

As we have seen, Scripture presents Jesus himself as the supreme example. The Bible also gives us Sarah, Abraham, Paul, Mary, and other women and men as excellent models. In addition, it gives definitions and pictures of the fruit of the Spirit.

However, getting a clear picture of what mature Christians are like is not as easy as it might seem. That's because our culture has definitions for words like love, which are not the same as the Christian understanding. Since the secular pictures are so vivid, often presented in living color and stereophonic sound, they are more accessible. The Christian definitions are harder to get at, requiring study, research, and careful observation, so we simply adopt the popular views, often quite unconsciously.

When we try to understand what the fruit of the Spirit are like, our pictures include elements that distort them. Our view of love, for example, may have been shaped as much by *Gone with the Wind* or the Beatles as by John's Gospel; our picture of joy by Walt Disney and various TV commercials more than by the Psalms; our understanding of peace by the six o'clock news more than the Letter to the Ephesians. So, I think it's a useful exercise to peel away the cultural elements from words like love, joy, peace, patience, and humility to get at the Christian meaning.

In the next eight chapters we will consider the fruit of the Spirit individually. When the contemporary culture has clouded the meaning of the quality or confused it with something less or something else, we will clear it up. In each case, we will look to Jesus, who is the perfect example of the fruit of the Spirit.

Love: 4
The Real Thing

Recently my wife and I went to see a film comedy about teenage romance. The evening was very educational. Mary Lou and I were at least twice as old as most people there and probably almost three times as old as half the audience. In other words, there were many fifteen-year-olds present.

This young audience was absorbing a powerful visual teaching about love. Before the credits rolled up over the closing scenes, in which the girl finally fell in love with the boy who had pursued her hotly across the celluloid for an hour and a half, the following points were driven home:

- Love and romance are synonyms.
- Love is something you fall into.
- Sexual love is the highest goal of life, at least for males.
- You cannot love someone you are not attracted to.
- Attraction and falling in love are stronger and more important than commitment.
- You should not have sex, unless you really love the person; that is, unless you are attracted to the person and have fallen in love with him or her.

I'm sure these messages were not news to anyone

viewing the film. They are the constant themes of movies, TV soaps, music videos, the Top 40, magazines, novels, Dear Abby columns, and so on. These are the ideas Americans already have in mind when they think about love.

THE REAL THING

What is Christian love really like? Let's look at one of the best pictures of love the Bible gives us. Even without the help of the wide screen and stereophonic sounds, the events of John 13 are very dramatic. It is the familiar story of the Last Supper. During the meal Jesus took off his outer garments, tied a towel around his waist, and with a basin of water began to wash the feet of his disciples.

We can almost hear Peter objecting stubbornly, "Lord, what do you mean trying to wash my feet!"

When Peter persisted, Jesus warned him, "If I do not wash you, you have no part in me." With typical extremism, Peter then begged the Lord to bathe him all over.

After he finished washing the disciples' feet, Jesus put his cloak back on, took his place at the meal, and said, "Do you know what I have done to you? You call me Teacher and Lord; and you are right, for so I am. If I then, your Lord and Teacher, have washed your feet, you also ought to wash one another's feet. For I have given you an example, that you also should do as I have done to you" (John 13:12-15 / RSV). Before the meal was over, Jesus completed his instruction by giving us all a new commandment that put words to the example: "A new commandment I give to you, that you love one another; even as I have loved you, that you also love one another" (John 13:34 / RSV).

He also said during that meal, "Greater love has no man than this, that a man lay down his life for his friends" (John 15:13 / RSV). The very next day he gave a living example by freely embracing death on the cross for us.

What does Jesus teach us here about Christian love? The main elements are:

- Christian love is not based on attraction or desire.
- Love is a commandment and a commitment.
- Love means serving and caring for others.
- Love is selflessly concerned for the interests of others.

Clearly, Jesus called for a love that is different in kind from the romantic love celebrated by our culture. *Eros*, the Greek word for the love between men and women, does not even appear in the New Testament. Now, Jesus did not condemn romance, but neither did he make romantic love the Christian ideal. However, Jesus did outlaw some practices our culture normally associates with romance, such as fornicating with someone, even if you "love" that person.

Christian love is not based on attraction or desire. Romantic love is good. God made it that way. Erotic love is the appropriate fruit of attraction. It is rooted in and generates sexual desire, and it expects a loving response from the other. If we have confused romantic love with Christian love, we may be mistakenly reserving our love for those we are drawn to and for those who show signs of loving us. We may also be trying to stir up feelings of love, thinking that Jesus commanded us to feel attracted to others or to like them, but this is not the case.

Jesus' love was not grounded in his attraction to others. For example, he expressed love for those who executed him by forgiving them as he hung from the cross (Luke 23:34). Certainly, he did not find them attractive, but he loved them all the same.

Love is a commandment and a commitment. The new commandment to love others was the dominant theme of Jesus' last discourse (John 15:10, 12, 14, 17 / JB): "If you keep my *commandments* / you will remain in my *love,* / . . . This is my *commandment:* / *love* one another, / as I have loved you. / . . . You are my friends, / if you do what I *command* you. / . . . What I *command* you / is to *love* one another." (Emphasis mine.) Commandments . . . love; commandment . . . love; command . . . command . . . love. These words reverberate like a motif in a symphony.

Jesus left his followers no loopholes. If we say we are his disciples, there must be evidence in our lives that we are obeying this commandment. John says, "If any one says, 'I love God,' and hates his brother, he is a liar; for he who does not love his brother whom he has seen, cannot love God whom he has not seen" (1 John 4:20 / RSV).

As Christians, our love for others depends upon who we are and not upon whom we are loving. We are disciples of Jesus. From that relationship flows our commitment to love people; this makes our own relationships resilient.

For example, I love my children because I am a follower of Jesus, not because they are nice, nor because they deserve to be loved. Honestly, there are times when I don't like my children much, because of their bad behavior. Have you ever known parents who were tempted to say with Bill Cosby's mother, "I brought you into this world and I can take you out of it"? I have felt that way. Let's face it, sometimes children are not nice, and parents feel as though they deserve rejection. But parents love them by decision.

If love depended upon whom we loved, we would not love much. However, we are free to love others, regardless of who they are, because love is a commandment that we are committed to obey.

Love means serving and caring for others. Love is practical. It is measured more by our consistent self-giving than by depth of feeling. However, this does not mean love is supposed to be cold or calculating, for it should be expressed warmly and affectionately.

Ever since I was twelve years old I have noticed with awe expressions of real love in my life. For example, I will never forget the way my mother's brothers and sisters responded to my father's early death. Even before his body was removed from our house after his fatal heart attack, they were all there, comforting, helping, caring for us children. For at least a year, sisters and sisters-in-law seemed daily to be in and out of our house, talking to Mother, bringing meals, and pitching in wherever they could. One brother visited every Sunday night for several years to provide fatherly attention to us boys. Another brother employed Mother when the family business had to fold. For many years all the uncles, aunts, and cousins gathered at our house on Christ-

30

mas Day, which was their way of filling up the emptiness my mother felt in that season. Their care was a school of love for me.

Love is selflessly concerned for the interests of others. Romantic love focuses attention on the beloved, but it also has a strong selfish element. While love songs, for example, praise the qualities of the one who is loved, they invariably carry themes like "I need you" or "I can't live without you." Lovers may strive to assure that their intimacy is mutually sensitive, but no matter how generous they are, the power of sexual desire drives them to seek their own gratification. How many lovers' quarrels spring from a failure to express affection or from a denial of intimacy?

There is nothing selfish, however, about Christian love. It asks not "What can I get out of it?" but rather "What can I put into it?" Jesus, the archetype of love, had nothing to gain in his public ministry. He gave his all for us at great personal cost.

A LOVE STORY

Love impelled Jim Elliot, a Protestant missionary who wanted more than anything else to bring the Gospel to people who had no way of knowing Jesus. His story is an inspiring illustration of the way charity works in the Christian life.[2] He graduated from Wheaton College in 1949 and eventually decided that God wanted him to enter the mission field among the Indians of Ecuador. He felt a strong desire to reach the Aucas, a small Stone Age tribe he had learned about in 1950 at a language institute.

However, from 1952 to 1956, Jim and his associate

Pete Fleming worked among the Quichua Indians, a much larger and more widespread tribe. The men built a mission center — complete with school, clinic, and an airstrip — at a place called Shandia. They struggled with the difficult Quichua language. The work of evangelizing these Indians went much more slowly than they had anticipated.

Jim continued to be fascinated with the idea of bringing the Gospel to the Aucas. He surveyed the jungle by air and seized every opportunity to search for Auca dwellings. He once wrote home, "We were looking for Auca homes as well, but found nothing. . . . More and more that tribe is brought before me as a possible field of labor for my life. . . . It would take a miracle to open the way to them, and we are praying for that miracle. They may be only a few hundred in number, but they are part of the whole creation, and we have orders for such."

In October, 1953, Jim married Elisabeth Howard, another missionary he had met at Wheaton. For the next two years they worked together among the Quichuas, establishing new outposts, translating the Sacred Scriptures into the Quichua language, and helping the people come to Christ. The native church grew steadily. A daughter, Valerie, was born to Elisabeth and Jim on February 27, 1955.

In September, 1955, word came from Nate Saint and Ed McCully, two other missionaries, that they had located an Auca settlement. Elisabeth says that from the instant the news arrived, Jim had one foot in the stirrup. The men prayed more fervently for a chance to bring the good news to the Aucas. They made weekly flights over the Auca houses for a period of five months, dropping gifts of machetes, kettles, and ribbons and calling out greetings in the few Auca words they knew. By January, 1956, they felt the time was right and five men set up camp on the banks of the Curaray River near the Auca settlement. Another missionary, Roger Youderian, had joined the original four.

On January 8, they flew over the Auca houses, inviting the Indians to come and meet them on the beach. Ten Auca men were spotted heading toward the camp and the men radioed their wives about the anticipated meeting. They were supposed to call back at 4:30 P.M. that day. The call never came. The men were found four days later, speared and scattered on the sand.

The story made big but brief news in the United States, including a spread in *Life* magazine. However, as the world turned its attention to other events, Elisabeth and the other women quietly continued their husbands' work. Jim's death prompted Elisabeth to pray for and to seek a way to bring the Gospel to the Aucas. She told a journalist, "The fact that Jesus Christ died for all makes me interested in the salvation of all, but the fact that Jim loved and died for the Aucas intensifies my love for them."

Her prayers were answered. Three Auca women who lived among the Quichuas invited Elisabeth to come to the the Auca settlement. In October, 1958, she (with her three-year-old daughter and Rachel Saint, Nate's sister) moved to the village where her husband's killers lived. They lived in a tiny open hut with hammocks for sleeping and an open pit for cooking. Elisabeth and Rachel worked to translate the New

Testament into the Auca language and befriended the people, trying to teach them about the Lord. After two years Elisabeth returned to work among the Quichuas and Rachel stayed on. Eventually a number of Aucas became Christians, including the six men who had killed Jim Elliot and his companions. One of these men became pastor of the Auca church and another was martyred himself in an attempt to take the Gospel to another Auca group.

Love had inspired Jim Elliot to seek out the Aucas and that love cost him his life. Love moved Elisabeth Elliot to find a way to bring Jesus to the Aucas and love found a way. Only a few of us will have the chance to express our love by working with people who have never heard about Christ. Fewer still will have a chance to join Jim Elliot in the high call of giving our lives for Christ.

The Lord, however, has invited all of us to spend our lives loving others in ways that cost us. We lose our life bit by bit when we serve someone else with time we had reserved for ourselves. When we help a needy friend with money we were stashing to treat ourselves, we die a little. The little daily acts of love that chip away at our lives are not very dramatic nor newsworthy, but as they accumulate they add up to heroism. With Jim Elliot, the Christian who loves can say, "He is no fool who gives what he cannot keep to gain what he cannot lose."

Goodness, Kindness, and Mercy 5

✓ Every day Mr. Martínez takes time out from his work to visit briefly with María, the senile old woman who lives next door. María is disoriented and often depressed; her conversation makes little sense. Mr. Martínez is always patient, has some encouragement for her, and now and then a little gift. If he's not there for some reason, María misses him, for he is a stable point in her disintegrated life.

✓ A little over twelve years ago I moved my family to Ann Arbor, Michigan. On the day we arrived with two huge vans, Dan, our new next-door neighbor, set up his charcoal grill and served hot dogs, snacks, and lemonade to all the helpers. That was only the first of many loving things Dan did for me and my family. Years later when we were packing to leave Ann Arbor for Florida, Dan was there every day of our final two weeks, helping pack pictures, putting up garage sale signs, and just being a friend. I did not know it at the time, but his stomach cancer was already accelerating and he died not long after we moved away.

✓ Catherine, Sally, and Maura are young women who became pregnant as unmarried teens. A family with six children welcomed them, making it possible for them to have their babies in a supportive place. Two of the women placed their children up for adoption; Sally kept her child and is now happily married. She still visits her "adopted" family, enjoying the volunteer grandparents, uncles, and aunts.

Goodness is Scripture's name for the quality displayed in these three true vignettes. Paul lists it as a fruit of the Spirit (Galatians 5:22). Goodness is closely related to kindness and mercy, both also regarded as fruit of the Spirit (Galatians 5:22 and Colossians 3:13). Sometimes Scripture uses the words interchangeably for the same kinds of deeds. Our reflection on these three qualities will broaden our understanding of love, for they are aspects of love in action.

Contemporary culture has not distorted the words good and goodness, so we need not clear our minds to grasp the Christian meaning. In ordinary speech something is good if it produces a state of well-being, and goodness is the ability to evoke that condition. For the Christian, the meaning is similar, with the distinction that our goodness is rooted in our relationship with God and is transmitted to us by the power of the Holy Spirit. Paul said, "We know that by turning everything to their good God co-operates with all those who love him, with all those that he has called according to his purpose" (Romans 8:28 / JB).[3]

THE GOODNESS OF JESUS

Anyone who saw Jesus, noticed his radical goodness. Jesus never seems to have thought of himself. We always find him caring for someone else. Even when he would finally be about to get some rest, someone would show up with a need.

Jesus spent himself generously for others. If we are tempted to think that it was easy for him, we should reconsider. Jesus was fully a man, flesh and blood like us. The crowd pressed him, draining his strength. He grew weary praying for the sick, but he healed all who came to him.

Even as Jesus hung from the cross — bruised, lacerated, nearly asphyxiated, racked with pain — he placed the interests of others ahead of his own. He looked down and saw Mary, his mother, and the disciple he was especially fond of. Intense throbs of pain could not prevent his one last act of generosity. "Woman," he said to Mary, "this is your son," and to the disciple, "This is your mother." Shortly after he asked his friend to care for his mother, Jesus died (John 19:25-27 / JB).

We can pick out three distinctive qualities here. Jesus' goodness was:

- Generous. Jesus did not hedge his goodness with protective shields, setting limits on his acts of kindness. He gave full measures of love, pressed down and running over.
- Consistent. Jesus never failed to act out of goodness. Nothing stopped him, including weariness, opposition, or fear.
- Inclusive. Jesus' goodness extended to everyone. He excluded no one.

These attributes must also mark our goodness. Paul said, "We must never get tired of doing good because if we don't give up the struggle we shall get our harvest at the proper time. While we have the chance, we must do good to all, and especially to our brothers in the faith" (Galatians 6:9-10 / JB).

One morning as Jesus was teaching the people in the Temple, scribes and Pharisees brought to him a woman who had been caught committing adultery (John 8:1-11 / RSV). Shamed and numbed with fear, she was forced to stand in front of everybody. Jesus' opponents hoped to trap him. They told Jesus that Moses had ordered them to condemn adulterous women to death by stoning, and asked if he had anything to say about it.

But Jesus said nothing. He bent down and began to write on the ground with his finger. That's one of the details that gives John's Gospel the ring of truth, but he does not tell us what the Lord wrote. Some speculate without evidence that he was listing the secret sins of the accusers.

"Well, what have you to say?" they persisted.

Jesus looked up and said, "Let him who is without sin among you be the first to throw a stone at her." Then he went back to writing on the ground.

Embarrassed and defeated, the accusers slipped away one by one until Jesus was left alone with the woman.

"Woman," Jesus said, "where are they? Has no one condemned you?"

"No one, Lord," she replied.

"Neither do I condemn you," said Jesus; "go, and do not sin again."

The woman in this account was in a terrible spot, facing what was probably the most difficult moment of her life. Were some of the overconfident accusers already carrying stones? What consideration could she expect from this itinerant preacher they were consulting about her case? He would certainly agree with their judgment.

But to her surprise he dismisses her accusers with his mysterious writing and inspired words. He neutralizes her shame by refusing to condemn her. Instead of letting her be crushed by the full force of legal justice, he releases her in an act of kindness that sparkles with love.

I selected this event as an illustration of the kindness of Jesus, but I could have presented it as an example of his goodness or his mercy. The boundaries that define these traits overlap, making them hard to distinguish. However, Jesus' conduct here closely resembles God's kindness toward his people in the Old Testament. The Greek word for this trait, *chrestotes*, expresses God's constant readiness to act benevolently toward his people. God remains unflinchingly kind (*chrestos*) to his people even when they have sinned (Jeremiah 33:11). Paul also used this word for kindness in the New Testament listing of the fruit of the Spirit (Galatians 5:22 and Colossians 3:12).[4]

Jesus' kindness to the woman highlights a significant characteristic of Christian love. Jesus was kind to the woman without requiring anything of her. She was guilty of serious wrongdoing, yet he acted in her behalf. Christian love is like that. It is unconditional.

God the Father in the Old Testament and Jesus in the New Testament gave generously without demanding anything in return. They were indiscriminate in showing kindness even to people who had declared themselves enemies. The Lord wants us to have the same unconditional love, acting kindly to all people, including those who hate us. "Love your enemies," he said, then he spelled out exactly what he meant:

- do good to those who hate you,
- bless those who curse you,
- pray for those who treat you badly.
- To the man who slaps you on one cheek, present the other cheek too;
- to the man who takes your cloak from you, do not refuse your tunic.
- Give to everyone who asks you,
- and do not ask for your property back from the man who robs you (Luke 6:27-30 / JB).

That's some checklist! Did you ever realize kindness was so hard? That it was so demanding? We don't feel like being kind to people who are hostile to us. If a person harms us, we ardently desire to return the "favor." Why, we sometimes find it hard to be kind to people we like. Isn't that the point? If we are to be kind even to enemies, then we must be kind to all. Aspiring to be like Christ means dying little deaths all the time. Having to be kind to everyone all the time will kill our self-indulgence by attrition.

MERCY

Once, a lawyer tried to disconcert Jesus by asking, "Master, what must I do to inherit eternal life?"

Anticipating his intent, Jesus turned the question back to him: "What is written in the law?"

The lawyer replied, " 'You must love the Lord your God with all your heart, with all your soul, with all your strength, and with all your mind, and your neighbor as yourself.' "

"You have answered right," said Jesus. "Do this and life is yours."

The lawyer did not want to appear to have asked a stupid question, so to save face he persisted. "And who is my neighbor?" he asked.

Jesus responded with a parable about a man who was robbed, beaten up by thugs, and left to die by the side of the road. Two fellow countrymen, both religious men presumably aware of their obligations to others, noticed him and passed by on the other side. Was it that they had more important things to do? Were they afraid for themselves? Perhaps they did not feel like getting involved. Whatever the reason, both behaved selfishly and left the man dying.

Who stopped? A Samaritan — an alien and a heretic! Not someone who you would expect to help a Jew in distress. Jesus said the Samaritan traveler "was moved with compassion when he saw him." He tended to the victim's wounds, carried him on his own mount to an inn, and arranged for his care, agreeing to cover any extra expenses upon his return.

At this point Jesus may have paused briefly, looked directly at the lawyer, and asked, "Which of these three, do you think, proved himself a neighbor to the man who fell into the brigands' hands?"

"The one who took pity on him," he replied.

Jesus said to him, "Go, and do the same yourself." (Based on Luke 10:25-37 / JB.)

Mercy is love in action. The word seems to be a more compelling term than either goodness or kindness, the strongest of the strong. More than the others, it seems, mercy works on two fronts. Internally, as compassion, mercy stirs the heart, evoking sympathy and a desire to act. Externally, mercy is our response, as we come to the aid of someone in need. In the parable the Samaritan was merciful in both senses. Overcome with compassion, he had mercy on the wounded man by rescuing him and taking care of him.

In the Old Testament, mercy frequently represents the Hebrew *hesed*, a word that stands for God's covenant loyalty to his people. The Lord stands with his people no matter what, graciously meeting their material and spiritual needs.[5] This is the root idea behind the mercy the Lord wants to produce in our character.

We have experienced the mercy of God, the same compassion the Lord showed in his tenderness for Israel. Paul said, "But God, who is rich in mercy, out of the great love with which he loved us, even when we were dead through our trespasses, made us alive together with Christ (by grace you have been saved), and raised us up with him, and made us sit with him in the heavenly places in Christ Jesus" (Ephesians 2:4-6 / RSV). Having received mercy from God, he expects us to have compassion on others. Jesus stated this principle for Christian living: "Be merciful, even as your Father is merciful" (Luke 6:36 / RSV).

JOSEPH'S STORY

At age four, after a sledding accident, a young man named Joseph was found to have tuberculosis of the spine. He endured casts, a spinal graft, and many years of lying strapped to a canvas board. However, in spite of all efforts, Joseph was left with a deformity. He wore a steel brace that concealed the hump in the middle of his back, but he himself was always conscious of the defect. A constant feeling of physical inferiority ate at him.

Joseph was always careful that no one saw him undress, but that privacy was about to be interrupted. The seventh-grade class in his private school was lined up for physical examinations. Very shortly a doctor was going to examine him. He dreaded it. However, he need not have feared, for the doctor was about to show him an act of mercy that would change the boy's life.

When Joseph entered the examining room, the doctor was reading his chart. His penetrating blue eyes seemed to look right into the lad, reading his pain and insecurity. He weighed the boy, measured his height, and then came the long-expected "Now, take that robe off." Joseph slipped nervously out of the garment and stood there hating himself.

Then the doctor approached Joseph, took the boy's face in his hands, and asked: "Do you believe in God?"

The question surprised him, but Joseph replied, "Yes, sir."

"That's good," the doctor said, "because there's nothing we can do in this world alone. The more faith we have in him, the greater the faith we have in ourselves."

"Yes, sir," Joseph said again.

Then after writing something on Joseph's chart the doctor excused himself from the room, saying he would be right back. Prompted by curiosity about what the doctor said regarding his deformity, Joseph glanced at the chart he had left on the desk. The doctor had recorded five words and nothing else: "Has an unusually well-shaped head." The boy was astonished at what he read. No mention of any deformity — just a compliment.

When he returned smiling, Joseph met his eyes and scampered from the room saying "Thank you, thank you, thank you." Joseph had got the message the doctor intended him to get — always look for the positive angle that turns difficulty to advantage. Joseph never forgot the doctor's little kindness; many years later he wrote about how it made a lifelong difference in his self-concept.[6]

Let's go and do the same. Who knows how far a kind word or deed will go?

Joy: Always with Us 6

America wears its heart on its bumpers. Slogans, mottos, one-liners, put-downs — sayings of all sorts are emblazoned on the rear ends of our cars. Usually witty or smug, sometimes wise, often vulgar or suggestive, bumper stickers express common themes. Perhaps most frequently seen are expressions of the universal desire for pleasure. Ever since someone wrote "I 'heart' New York," people have been "hearting" everything they delight in, from their goldfish to their hairdresser.

Some find their fun in possessions: "Shop till you drop." Others in wildness, sex, drink, or drugs: "Get high and stay high." Or, "I need someone really bad. Are you really bad?" Old and young have their own versions: many Florida drivers, for example, either declare that they're "sexy senior citizens" or urge you to "surf naked."

I think it's a sign of hope that many of these bumper stickers are tongue-in-cheek, indicating that we don't really believe that pleasure satisfies. For example, one current banner questions rampant materialism: "The one who dies with the most toys wins." My teenaged daughter, Elaine, has two slogans on her car: "Let's party!" and "Are we having fun yet?" I like the ambivalence because it recognizes that fun is good, but it's not the ultimate answer.

Fun, pleasure, and happiness are good in themselves. They go bad only when we abuse them, like making them the goal of our lives, a position they were never intended to hold. God put in us the capacity to enjoy life, and Jesus himself showed that it is all right to have fun. For example, he enjoyed parties at Levi's house and at the wedding at Cana, where he even miraculously supplied some of the refreshments.

Pleasure and happiness resemble joy, the Christian quality that we call a fruit of the Spirit. For example, they produce a feeling of gladness in us, just as joy does. However, pleasure and happiness have limits that distinguish them from joy. Unlike joy, which has a better source, they originate in things we do or acquire. We get pleasure from recreation or from being with friends. A child is delighted with a new toy, and Daddy with a new car. We are happy when we graduate from school or when we are promoted at work.

Pleasure and happiness are by nature oriented to the self. They can be self-seeking in a healthy sense. Contentment, for example, centers on the self, and there is nothing wrong with it when our lives are in good order. Fun, relaxation, and humor are essential saving graces in intense, overcommitted lives. It's only when we orient our lives to the pursuit of pleasure for its own sake that it gets bent out of shape and may become wickedly selfish.

People find out quickly that pleasure is temporary and only partially fulfilling; their daily experience proves that happiness is elusive. While pleasure makes us feel good, the feeling soon fades. The happiness we experience over an achievement evaporates too quickly.

We must accomplish something else to feel happy again. We have a burning desire for a joy that satisfies and stays.

When good feelings don't come frequently enough, or when misery engulfs them, which for many is a daily occurrence, people may resort to producing pleasure with chemicals like alcohol or drugs. Or they go on other kinds of binges. As the bumper sticker says, "When the going gets tough, the tough go shopping." Or eating. Or sleeping. Or watching TV. Or finding some other escape from the pain. I have learned to be slow to criticize people who soothe themselves with addictions. They are looking for a cure to a deep longing, one that God put in them, and they have not yet received it.

Charley Reese, a columnist in our local paper, recently wrote about the reason people use drugs.[7] People turn to drugs, which alter the perception of reality, in order to escape their perception of the reality of their lives. Reese says Americans are unhappy because their lives are void of real meaning and he correctly diagnoses a spiritual problem. "The fatal flaw [in American materialism] is that it dodges completely the tough question all great religions face squarely — man's mortality and all the sorrow that it unavoidably entails. . . . Man's lot on earth is essentially unhappy and we all know it. . . . When the only answer to the question — What is my life all about? — is drive a nice car and drink Michelob and invest in a good mutual fund, the result is equally disastrous to those who can never hope to drive a good car and to those who can."

The relevant bumper sticker here is "Life is rotten, and then you die."

Joy is what we're looking for, a perfection of pleasure, of happiness that shines through darkness, that wells up with gladness, that soothes with healing, delight, and fullness. We can see it in Jesus himself, and learn about it from his teaching.

In Luke 10 we are told that Jesus once sent seventy disciples, two by two, to every town he intended to visit. He instructed them to preach the coming of the kingdom of God and he authorized them to act in his behalf. Luke records that the seventy returned with joy, celebrating the fact that even demons obeyed them when they invoked Jesus.

The Lord was excited to greet them when they came back. The Holy Spirit had given him an advance report of their effectiveness. He knew they had done well and he was glad. We can imagine the joyful scene when he welcomed them. They would have been shouting and laughing, embracing and slapping each other on the back. There would have been more real joy in that homecoming than in any celebration over a candidate's election or an athletic team's victory.

"I saw Satan fall," Jesus told them, "like lightning from heaven." Then he warned them not to let the whole thing go to their heads. "Do not rejoice in this, that spirits are subject to you; but rejoice that your names are written in heaven." The disciples were to rejoice more in their union with God than in their evangelistic successes. Jesus expressed his own gladness by worshiping his Father. Luke says that he was "filled with the joy of the Holy Spirit" and thanked God for revealing these realities to ordinary people. One paraphrase of this passage says that "Jesus leapt for joy."

Jesus shows us here some key elements of joy:
- The source of joy is a relationship with God.
- The Holy Spirit produces joy in us.
- Joy causes internal feelings of gladness that we can express externally.
- Worship is an appropriate expression of joy.
- Experiencing salvation, either our own or someone else's, occasions joy.
- Christian service, especially bringing others to Christ, promotes joy.

Christian joy is different in kind from pleasure, even though it has similar effects, such as good feelings. Pleasure is circumstantial, coming from events or our actions, but we get joy from our union with Christ, and circumstances merely enhance it. At the Last Supper Jesus said that if we abide in him, as a branch draws life from the vine, and if we obey him, we will have perfect joy. "These things I have spoken to you," he said, "that my joy may be in you, and that your joy may be full" (John 15:11 / RSV). That night he also prayed that we would have his joy fulfilled in ourselves (John 17:13).

Just as the Holy Spirit inspired joy in the Lord, he is the cause of our joy. When we were spiritually dead through sin, we had no principle of joy in us. But now because we are reborn in Christ, the Holy Spirit (the principle of new life in us) makes us joyful. So Paul lists joy as one of the fruit of the Spirit (Galatians 5:22).

Unlike pleasure, which is incomplete, elusive, and temporary, real joy is full, substantial, and durable. Because we are in Christ, we find ourselves in a fundamentally good situation, so our underlying disposition can be joyful. As Peter said: "Without having seen him you love him; though you do not now see him you believe in him and rejoice with unutterable and exalted joy" (1 Peter 1:8 / RSV).

Because joy endures, coursing through our lives like deep channel springs in a river, Paul can freely command us to always be joyful (1 Thessalonians 5:16) and to rejoice at all times in the Lord (Philippians 4:4). Otherwise those would be hollow orders, directing us to pretend happiness in the face of disaster, to fake gladness in misery.

JOY AMID TRIALS

When things are going bad and we are unhappy, we may not feel very joyful. Sometimes we seem to have no joy flowing throughout our lives because circumstances have somehow blocked the way. When we are suffering we must do what we can to stimulate joy, for it is there to buoy us up and carry us through hardship. Frankly, at those times, it is very hard to feel joy. Scripture says that Jesus endured the savagery of the cross, looking forward to the joy that would be his; it does not say that his anticipating the promise eliminated the pain (Hebrews 12:2). The hope of joy made the agony more endurable. James said, "Count it all joy, my brethren, when you meet various trials, for you know that the testing of your faith produces steadfastness" (James 1:2 / RSV).

Recall the little band of Christians in Jerusalem, just after the Church was founded. The group huddled in fear, waiting to see what the authorities would do with John and Peter who had been arrested for healing a lame man. The two were released. When they returned to their comrades, that handful of men and women, who should have been horror-stricken, prayed not for escape but for more miracles. Their joyful praise, inspired by the Holy Spirit, rocked the house (Acts 4:31).

Today's Christians can still count on joy to sustain them through trials. Consider the story of Kathryn Koob.

For four hundred forty-four days — from November 4, 1979, until January 20, 1981 — the threat of imminent death hung over Kathryn Koob and sixty-five others who had been taken hostage in Teheran by Iranians.[8] In a few short hours on that fateful day, November 4, 1979, her normal life as director of the Iran-America Society had become a nightmare of terror and desperation.

These fourteen and a half months were difficult for Kathryn Koob, and they could not be described as joyful. Yet joy was a resource that helped her get through her trial. She did everything she could to tap into its power. She recalled all the hymns she could remember — about a half an hour's worth. She found strength every day as she sang of God's love and faithfulness and of her surrender: "Have thine own way, Lord, have thine own way. Thou art the potter; I am the clay."

Kathryn lived one day at a time, believing that God was a pillar of support for her. She expressed thanks amid evil circumstances, "Lord, you have given me this day, and I give it back to you." She read her little New Testament repeatedly, marking passages that promised hope. She interceded for her family, for Christians everywhere, and for her fellow hostages. One night as she

51

lay on her blanket on the floor, she begged God, "Lord, this has been a rough day. I don't know. Can you tell me something?" As she opened her hymnal, she read a verse that would sustain her for the duration of her trial. "I shall not die, but I shall live, / and recount the deeds of the LORD. The LORD has chastened me sorely, / but he has not given me over to death" (Psalm 118:17-18 / RSV). She knew at once that God would deliver her from her imprisonment. Months later, shortly after midday on January 20, 1981, Kathryn Koob and the other hostages left the Teheran airport on a plane bound for home.

Nothing makes us feel less like being joyful than trouble or opposition. Paradoxically, in moments of suffering, our joy can serve us most by making us resilient, for joy is the companion of perseverance and courage.

THE FRUIT OF WORSHIP

Joy is not something we can get on our own. We cannot give it to ourselves. If we try for it too hard, we will have to settle for something less or for a counterfeit. Joy comes from God. The best way to receive it is to come before the Lord in prayer.

Anne Sandberg, for example, says that she lived a joyless Christian life until she learned to worship in God's presence.[9] As a girl of eighteen, Anne was pressured by her older sisters to stay at home to help her mother raise her two younger brothers. The desire of Anne's heart was to be married, but she postponed that, out of love for her family. As the years piled up and marriage seemed less likely, she grew more lonely, more resentful, and more unhappy. When she came across passages such as "In thy presence there is fulness of joy" (Psalm 16:11 / RSV), she was at once attracted and repelled by them, for they seemed so contradictory to her own experience.

Something began to change for Anne when, at age thirty-one, she moved into the home of a young pastor and his wife to assist them in doing youth work. "Mornings we prayed together," she wrote. "After a while I noticed something. I always began petitioning; they knelt, silent, faces upturned, worshiping. With awe I watched their radiant faces, heard them murmur, 'I love you, Jesus. . . .'" The young pastor kindly taught Anne to worship. He gave her a little book by Andrew Murray, *Waiting on God*.

"Read a little, then meditate in silence, keeping your attention on Jesus," he said. "When your mind wanders, read a little more, then look at Jesus. Get really acquainted with him. Be with him."

Anne did not find the new effort at meditative worship easy. Her mind wandered; distractions barraged her, but she kept at it faithfully every day.

Many years later, she wrote: "Slowly I entered a new spiritual dimension. Like a flower turned toward the sun, my heart responded to Jesus' love. In about a year and a half I found myself looking forward to the hour of sitting at the feet of Jesus and looking into his face. The pangs of loneliness became less frequent, less painful; envy of married couples decreased. . . .

"One day as I waited on God, I realized that something wonderful had happened to me. His presence filled my being and I could say from my heart, 'Whom have I in heaven but thee? And there is nothing upon earth that I desire besides thee' (Psalm 73:25). And I wept with joy."

Anne Sandberg's life had made a one-hundred-eighty-degree turn. She continued her Christian service, married a dedicated Christian man, and raised two daughters, one born to the couple and a foster daughter. At age forty-five she was widowed. She wrote, "Despite the joy of being a wife and mother, I still found my highest happiness in Jesus. Nothing else was as wonderful as my quiet hour, sitting at the feet of Jesus, my beloved."

The more we worship God, the more joyful we will be.

Peace Bonds 7

Novelist Rex Stout's mother liked to read, a pastime she pursued with gusto. Like all beleaguered mothers, she only wanted some peace and quiet in which to snatch a little personal pleasure. You will admire that lady's determination and perhaps you may want to imitate the steps she took. Whenever she read, Mrs. Stout kept at hand a basin of ice water and a face cloth. When a child approached, she would pretend that his face was dirty and in need of a vigorous wiping. Soon she could read without interruption.

As the parents of seven (including four teenagers), my wife, Mary Lou, and I have our own quest for peace and quiet. Our sons, for example, cannot think clearly unless a radio is blasting violent noises into their heads. Since we are older and cannot even think when their electronic boxes are blasting, we have made some ground rules. For example, "Thou shalt not blast thy box in the living room, where others read or visit." So, we get a little quiet.

In a family of nine, peace is somewhat harder to come by. Have you ever watched a fifteen-year-old tormenting a two-year-old by hiding her doll? Or a seventeen-year-old driving an eleven-year-old to tears with teasing? Or how about an eleven-year-old entrapping a seventeen-year-old by screaming bloody murder just as Dad walks around the corner? Have you ever been forced to listen in as a ten-year-old and an eight-year-old exchanged put-downs on your front porch? "Okay!" shouts Dad, "I've had enough!" A few people get sent to bedrooms and others to different parts of the house. "And don't dare come out till I say so!" Ah, peace at last. For a little while.

THE CESSATION OF HOSTILITIES

This notion of peace is not very satisfying. It is elusive and temporary. It's hard to get and hard to keep. Peace as the absence of noise, confusion, or trouble seems exclusively negative.

The same is true for some popular ideas of world peace. From time immemorial, peace in the political realm has mainly meant the absence of war. This brand of peace, however, means only the cessation of hostilities, not the end of hostility. Even when the hot war shuts down, as we learned in the last generation, a cold war may rage on, erupting every so often in fierce localized explosions, like Korea and Vietnam.

As a young college professor in the 1960s, I opposed the war in Vietnam. I associated with others in our town who were working for peace. We studied about the war, gave talks, held prayer meetings, counseled students, signed petitions, made contributions, and so on. Whatever else you might say about us, we were genuinely pursuing peace, and we were taking what seemed to us to be constructive steps.

Then something nasty happened. When the students returned to campus one fall, many of the peacemakers seemed less interested in peace than in violence against those who were making war. True, the war was being escalated, and no one seemed to be listening to their call for peace, but that did not seem to justify behavior that denied the ideal we lived for. I was shocked at the ease with which peace was traded off for hostility.

As I reflected on the hardening of the peace movement, I decided that the peace I had been pursuing was good, but that somehow it was not quite the same as Christian peace. I had mistaken a part for the whole. The cessation of hostilities was an element in the peace of Christ, as affection had a part to play in Christian love. But just as affection was not the whole of love, I concluded that the same was true for political peace in relation to Christian peace.

'PEACE THAT PASSES ALL UNDERSTANDING'

At the Last Supper, Jesus said, "Peace I leave with you; my peace I give to you; not as the world gives do I give to you. Let not your hearts be troubled, neither let them be afraid. You heard me say to you, 'I go away, and I will come to you' " (John 14:27-28 / RSV). We can see here some of the distinctive elements of Christian peace:

- Christian peace is different in kind from the peace of the world. Paul calls it "peace that passes all understanding" (see Philippians 4:7).
- Jesus gives us his peace as a gift. It is not something we get for ourselves by work.
- Peace brings calm in the face of trouble and it overcomes fear.
- There is an identity between Christ himself and

57

peace. As Paul says, Christ "is our peace" (Ephesians 2:14 / RSV).

The passage above shows Jesus giving his disciples a farewell *shalom*, the ancient Jewish greeting. In biblical Israel, when you wished someone *shalom*, you were praying for a peace that went well beyond the cessation of hostilities. *Shalom* meant well-being, prosperity, and health untouched by violence or misfortune. It was also a harmony that came from living in unity with brothers and sisters under the Old Covenant. For the Israelite the word came to mean wholeness, a perfection in life and spirit that exceeded any success people could reach on their own.[10]

By his death and resurrection, Jesus gave us a peace that meant everything *shalom* did, and more. The peace of Christ was to be our reconciliation with God and the substance of unity in the New Israel, the Church.

For Christ "is our peace," Paul taught, "who has made us both one, and has broken down the dividing wall of hostility, . . . that he might create in himself one new man in place of the two, so making peace" (Ephesians 2:14-15 / RSV). Paul spoke here of the union of Jews and Gentiles in the body of Christ, which by extension refers to unity in the Church. By bringing people to himself, Jesus binds together in the Church various groups that have hated each other for centuries: slaves and masters, rich and poor, black people and white people, and even Orthodox, Protestant, and Roman Catholic, who are scandalously divided yet one in Christ.

Paul further explains that Christ established peace

and unity by destroying the wall of hostility, so that he "might reconcile us both to God in one body through the cross, thereby bringing the hostility to an end" (Ephesians 2:16 / RSV). While peace as we learn it in the world covers up hostility with a mere cessation, the peace that Christ gives puts an end to it.

MAINTAINING PEACE

Like all the fruit of the Spirit, peace is a trait produced in us by the action of the Holy Spirit. No matter how hard we try, we cannot cause it, nor can we make ourselves men and women of peace by striving after it. However, the Lord leaves us free to maintain peace or not, linking his strength to our weakness.

"If you go snapping at each other," Paul says, "and tearing each other to pieces, you had better watch or you will destroy the whole community" (Galatians 5:15 / JB). When evil desires have our ear, we tend to ruin relationships. We are selfish or greedy. We strive to be first. We ignore others' needs. We speak against each other. We snub people. We quarrel. So we must take seriously Paul's warning, and protect peace by refraining from any act that injures others.

We can also take positive steps to build peace. Paul exhorts us to do all we can to preserve the unity of the Spirit by the peace that binds us together (Ephesians 4:3). Constructive conduct that strengthens relationships involves loving acts such as:

- Encouraging others and expressing affection warmly. Supportive speech elicits trust and eliminates fear, enabling people to live and work together peaceably.

59

- Asking forgiveness when we've done something wrong, and freely forgiving someone who has hurt us. The hurt feelings and bitterness that come from unrepaired wrongs are the pilings that support new walls of hostility between us.
- Serving people in little ways that they will understand as expressions of love. In doing things for others, we prefer to do the things that we like to do; we must learn to do the things they prefer, whether we like to do them or not.

Jesus is the exemplary peacemaker. The disciples damaged their relationship with him by leaving him to face his death alone. They were doubly distressed, for the one they loved and hoped in was gone and they felt guilty because they had abandoned him.

However, the first thing Jesus did when he appeared to the disciples after he rose from the dead was to restore their relationship with him. "Peace be with you," he said, and to assure them that all was well, he repeated the greeting (John 20:21). There was substance to the peace Jesus offered to the disciples. Peace was the cure for their distress and sense of loss. Peace was their reunion with the Lord whom they had given up for dead and their restoration to the Master they had abandoned. Peace brought healing to their emotions and to their relationship with him.

In an early morning encounter, Jesus restored with supreme gentleness his relationship with Peter. Peter had denied him three times, once even swearing that he never knew the Lord. Jesus gave Peter three opportunities to declare his love afresh and then he affirmed Peter's leadership among the disciples (John 21:15-17).

Jesus is also our peace, reuniting us to himself and restoring our relationship to him. And the peace Jesus gives to us, he wants us to extend to others. "Blessed are the peacemakers," he taught, "for they shall be called sons of God" (Matthew 5:9 / RSV). We are marked with the peace of Christ when we bring people together in love and when we work to maintain good relationships.

Peace can work in the worst of circumstances, because peace has its source in God. The night before he died on the cross, Jesus spoke plainly to his disciples about his work among us: "I have said this to you, that in me you may have peace. In the world you have tribulation; but be of good cheer, I have overcome the world" (John 16:33 / RSV).

I am reminded of Corrie and Betsie ten Boom, two Dutch Christians who were imprisoned by the Nazis for concealing Jews during the Holocaust.

At the nadir of their agony, Corrie and Betsie were herded into Ravensbruck, a concentration camp where they were made to do forced labor. They were housed with fourteen hundred other women, many of them sick, in a flea-infested dormitory built for four hundred. Their suffering was unimaginable — it included illness, filth, stench, exhaustion, overcrowding, indignities, abuse, vulgarity, absence of privacy, and the constant torment of flea bites. The possibilities for hostility among the inmates were innumerable.

One night as brawls began to break out among the women, whose nerves had been gnawed thin by terror, Betsie prayed that Christ would send his peace into the room. Slowly the tension broke, and women who were about ready to break into fistfights began to laugh and joke with one another. Betsie and Corrie were able to be peacemakers among the women during these horrible days, especially keeping them from harming one another.[11] If the peace of Christ can bring calm to troubled people at places as hideous as Ravensbruck, this fruit of the Spirit has the strength to see us through any difficulty.

Patience: Proof of the Christian

8

In July, 1973, when Tom Bradley was sworn in as mayor of Los Angeles, almost fifty years had passed since his family had migrated from Calvert, Texas, to the big city, looking in vain for a better life. With one crisis after another, it had taken the seven sharecroppers most of 1924 to coax along their rattly old Ford Model T, crammed with all their possessions. City life turned out to be so bad for them that their father became disillusioned and abandoned the young family. All their hopes and dreams seemed to leave with him. Memories of many adverse years crowded Tom's thoughts as he made his inaugural speech as mayor. "It's been a long, long way for Tom Bradley," he said.

How does Tom explain his rags-to-riches success story? He credits two "built-in blessings": his mother and her ability to make God real to her family. Crenner Bradley was a woman with tenacity, pluck, and faith. She worked long hours during the day helping other families and long hours at night to care for her own. Poverty and hunger pursued the family relentlessly, but she never gave up. "My mother saw to it that we were never in despair," Tom said. "She made us feel that we had a Heavenly Father taking care of us, keeping us from harm, watching us when we did right, and when we did wrong. It was true that our [natural] father had left us, but, no sir, we Bradleys were not a father-less family."[12]

Some people might balk at the idea that Crenner Bradley was considered a model of Christian patience, but I think she was. Mrs. Bradley, they would argue, was everything but patient. She was not absolutely reconciled to her situation. She refused to accept circumstances submissively. She was active, determined, and impatient; she was not passive, resigned, and patient. They would be right about Crenner Bradley and wrong about patience.

There is a common misconception of patience that mistakenly identifies it with passivity and resignation. In this view, patient Christians are doormat Christians — they just lie there and take it. True, patience does involve accepting circumstances calmly, but to say patience equals resignation is to make the part the whole. Patience also involves other more active elements, such as persistence and determination, and therefore must not be reduced to passivity. Ironically, some of the qualities we associate with impatience actually belong to patience properly understood. Patience, for example, doggedly refuses to acquiesce in evil. Patience resists it and persists in doing good.

The view that sees patient Christians as doormat Christians misinterprets the Christian teaching on suffering. Yes, Christians can endure painful difficulties because they are looking forward to a heavenly reward, but to say that this renders them passive is a caricature. Patience accepts circumstances but refuses to wallow in idleness because it is built on hope. The theme of this well-known Scripture passage that compares the hope-filled Christian life to long-distance running is patience: "We . . . should throw off everything that hinders us, especially the sin that clings so easily, and keep running steadily in the race we have started. Let us not lose sight of Jesus, who leads us in our faith and brings it to perfection: for the sake of the joy which was still in the future, he endured the cross, disregarding the shamefulness of it, and *from now on has taken his place at the right* of God's throne" (Hebrews 12:1-2 / JB). Anyone who does even a modest amount of regular physical exercise would never say that patient endurance is entirely passive. For example, I begin my workday with aerobic exercises that require more stamina than anything else I do. The effort I must put out to keep at it, Scripture says, is like the persistence of patience.

FORBEARANCE

Imagine how the disciples must have frustrated Jesus. He spent three years teaching them and confiding his plans to them. He hoped they would understand, but they often missed the point. For example, on his first three tries to tell them about his imminent death, they showed how little they grasped. On the first occasion, Peter tried to talk him out of it (Mark 8:27-33). Just after his second attempt, Jesus had to correct the disciples for arguing over who was the greatest (Mark 9:31-35). James and John chose his third try to negotiate for high offices in his kingdom (Mark 10:32-40).

When they assembled at the Mount of Olives for their final meeting after the resurrection, Jesus might have expected that they would understand at last, but they didn't. "Lord," they asked, "will you at this time restore the kingdom to Israel?" (Acts 1:6 / RSV). Even then they were still preoccupied with a political kingdom.

The disciples' failures frustrated the Lord, but he always responded patiently. At the Last Supper, when Philip said, "Lord, let us see the Father and then we shall be satisfied," Jesus replied kindly, "Have I been with you all this time, Philip, and you still do not know me?" (John 14:8-9 / JB). Occasionally Jesus corrected his disciples sharply, but he never lashed out at them. Because he loved them he was determined to help them get it right, so he was willing to put up with their mistakes. If he got angry — and we know that he was capable of vigorous anger — he moderated it with patience.

Patience that bears with others' wrongs and weaknesses is called forbearance. When God revealed himself as "slow to anger" (Exodus 34:6), he was describing his forbearance, which is the pattern for the Christian virtue. The Father patiently restrained his wrath toward sinful people because he was determined to give them salvation. Peter, for example, explained the apparent delay of the Lord's Second Coming as an indication of God's forbearance that gave everyone an opportunity to repent (2 Peter 3:9).

Paul presents himself as living evidence for divine forbearance. He accounted his early opposition to Christianity as the worst blasphemy, making him the greatest of sinners. Paul tells us: "The saying is sure and worthy of full acceptance, that Christ Jesus came into the world to save sinners. And I am the foremost of sinners; but I received mercy for this reason, that in me, as the foremost, Jesus Christ might display his perfect patience for an example to those who were to believe in him for eternal life" (1 Timothy 1:15-16 / RSV).

In the parable of the unforgiving debtor (Matthew 18:23-35 / RSV) Jesus taught that our forgiveness and our patience must be like God's. When the king ordered the servant and his family sold to meet the debt, the servant appealed to his forbearance. "Lord," he begged, "have patience with me, and I will pay you everything." Moved with pity the king not only released his servant, but he also forgave the entire debt, which was the equivalent of millions of dollars. In his turn, the servant refused to forbear a fellow servant who owed him a few thousand dollars and who begged him to be patient. When the king found out, he unleased his wrath, jailing the servant until he should pay the debt he owed the king. The message is plain. Because our King has been patient and forgiving, we must be patient and forgiving too.

FOUR QUALITIES

Christian forbearance, based on God's patience with us, has four distinctive qualities:

✓ Long-suffering. Because it is a fruit of the Spirit, patience is made of strong, resilient stuff. It can put up with a lot. Meditating on the Lord's patience with me helps me to be patient with my family and friends. If he has borne so much from me, can I not exercise a little forbearance? "Bear with one another charitably," Paul says, "in complete selflessness, gentleness and patience" (Ephesians 4:2 / JB).

✓ Powerful. Patience has enough spiritual energy

to tame anger, one of our fiercest emotions. We must be like the Lord, who gets angry at our offenses but subdues his wrath to give us a chance to correct our course. Patience does not cancel out anger; instead, by grace, patience restrains it and enables us to channel its force into loving behavior. We can give people who offend us a chance by tempering our anger with forbearance.

√ Persistent. The Lord's patience has an element of dogged pursuit. He is resolved to win us and he never lets up. Our patience too must be marked by a determination to get things to go right. For example, Mary Lou and I are patient with our children, but that does not mean we tolerate all unacceptable behavior. When we see something wrong in one of them that must be corrected, we determine to keep at it until it changes.

√ Loving. Ancient Greek philosophers taught that people should cultivate patience for purely selfish interests, believing that tempered emotions occasioned personal happiness. In contrast, Christian patience is mainly oriented to helping us love others well. Paul makes patience a primary expression of love. He says, "Love is always patient and kind; . . . Love . . . is always ready to excuse, to trust, to hope, and to endure whatever comes" (1 Corinthians 13:4, 6 / JB).[13]

ENDURANCE AND PERSEVERANCE

"Someone has escaped!" The word quickly spread, striking terror into the hearts of the prisoners in Auschwitz cell block 14 during the night of July 30, 1941. They knew that the Nazis would exact swift vengeance: ten men would be selected on the following day for a slow death by starvation. Immediately after the escape was discovered the next morning, the entire cell block was made to stand at attention on the field. With almost no food or rest, they were kept there through the blistering heat until sundown when Deputy-Commander Fritsch of the Gestapo selected ten hostages who would be starved to death.

"My poor wife and children! I will never see them again!" said Sergeant Francis Gajowniczek, one of the choices. He lost control and wept openly. While all looked on in horror, another prisoner stepped forward and said, "I would like to take the place of Sergeant Gajowniczek."

"Who are you?" asked the deputy-commander.

"I am a Catholic priest," said the prisoner.

Fritsch didn't care, as long as he had ten hostages, so the priest was allowed to replace the sergeant. Prodded along by rifle butts, the ten were sealed in a bunker and left to die. "You will come out like dried-up tulip bulbs," a guard had mocked as they entered.

The priest was Maximilian Kolbe,[14] who along with hundreds of other Franciscan priests had generated a spiritual renewal movement among Polish Catholics between the First and Second World Wars. In his life and death, Kolbe stands as a model of Christian patience in adversity.

Afflicted by tuberculosis during most of his adult life, Kolbe was still able to perform tireless Christian service, building a far-reaching publications network to spread the Gospel. His tuberculosis was in high gear when he arrived at Auschwitz in May, 1941. Kolbe was made to haul heavy loads of gravel for the construction of the camp crematorium. Later the Nazis compelled him to carry corpses there. The guards could not comprehend Kolbe's calm spirit; they could not look him in the eye. They tried to break him by mockery, indignities, and beatings.

They failed. Kolbe was a source of encouragement and counsel to all. "No, no!" he was heard to say. "These Nazis will not kill our souls, since we prisoners certainly distinguish ourselves quite definitely from our tormentors; they will not be able to deprive us of the dignity of our Catholic belief. We will not give up. And when we die, then we die pure and peaceful, resigned to God in our hearts."

When exhaustion and disease forced the Nazis to hospitalize Kolbe, he continued to help others battle dehumanization and despair. A doctor imprisoned with him recalled: "Like many others, I crawled at night in the infirmary on the bare floor to the bed of Father Maximilian. . . . 'Hatred is not creative,' he whispered to me. . . . His reflections on the mercy of God went straight to my heart. His words to forgive the persecutors and to overcome evil with good kept me from collapsing into despair."

Kolbe's presence made his starvation bunker unlike any other. He prayed and sang aloud, and influenced the men to join him. Another prisoner, whose duty was removing dead bodies from bunkers, said: "Father never complained. . . . When his fellow prisoners, writhing in agony, were begging for a drop of water, and in despair were screaming and cursing, Father Kolbe would calm them down, inspiring them to perseverance."

Kolbe and three others survived into the third week in the starvation bunker. Impatient to kill them, the Nazis ordered the camp executioner to inject them with carbolic acid, which he did on the night of August 14, 1941. (In 1982, Maximilian Kolbe was recognized as a saint, according to the canons of the Roman Catholic Church.)

Patience that equips us to handle difficulties is called endurance or perservance. It is the steadfastness to withstand whatever comes. In describing the end times, Jesus spoke of wars, famine, earthquakes, persecution, animosity, apostasy, and lawlessness. "And because wickedness is multiplied, most men's love will grow cold. But he who endures to the end will be saved" (Matthew 24:12-13 / RSV).

Daily we are barraged with trials and difficulties ranging from the small to the large economy size. Patience is the ability to stand up amid no matter what hits us and to stay standing through it all to the end. Jesus himself is the supreme model of steadfastness. "Let us not lose sight of Jesus, who leads us in our faith and brings it to perfection: for the sake of the joy which was still in the future, he endured the cross, disregarding the shamefulness of it, . . . Think of the way he stood such opposition from sinners and then you will not give up for want of courage. In the fight against sin, you have not yet had to keep fighting to the point of death" (Hebrews 12:2-4 / JB).

Patience is also a steady persistence in doing good in all circumstances. On one hand, patience acts on our behalf, protecting us when harm threatens; on the other, patience enables us to act in behalf of others. Paul says God will reward with eternal life "those who by patience in well-doing seek for glory and honor and immortality" (Romans 2:7 / RSV). Again Jesus is our best example. Even as he hung dying on the cross, he served others: he forgave his executioners, he had mercy on the good thief, and he asked the beloved disciple to care for his mother.

THE PROOF

Trials can play a big role in our Christian growth, depending on our response. Even little daily nuisances can help us become more like Christ and more effective in his service, if we'll let them.

Carolyn, the art and production director in the publishing company where I work, has a thankless job. She is responsible for supervising the preparation of magazines and books for printers, and so she must depend on many things going right all the time. Few things do. People miss deadlines, copy does not fit on a page, an advertisement does not arrive, a mistake must be corrected at the last minute, the color is not right, the press is down, the magazines are sent to the wrong post office — so goes the litany of difficult circumstances.

I have worked alongside Carolyn for more than a year and I have never seen her lose patience in the midst of the daily pressures. Frustration could provoke drastic actions — fire someone, get a new printer, and so on. Carolyn, however, always calm, manages to solve the problem. Unruffled, she finds good amid the mess of little evils. Watching her go through a day is a real lesson in patience for me.

Carolyn could easily be overwhelmed by circumstances, drowned in a sea of petty nuisances. Instead, she endures, making her way patiently through them.

Mature Christians are supposed to be this way — tested by trials so that they are no longer overwhelmed by them, but proven in their ability to master them. James says, "Count it all joy, my brethren, when you meet various trials, for you know that the testing of your faith produces steadfastness. And let steadfastness have its full effect, that you may be perfect and complete, lacking in nothing" (James 1:2-4 / RSV). When circumstances direct our lives, we can accomplish little; but when we have acquired patience, we can do much good, serving the Lord and others.

Faithfulness: Doing What Is True

9

Rex Stout's fat detective genius, Nero Wolfe, is eccentric and pigheaded. Archie Goodwin, his streetwise associate and man Friday, says that if Wolfe ever decided to stop detecting he could hire himself out to a physics lab as an immovable object. One of Archie's responsibilities is jogging Wolfe out of his lethargy, an inertia that idles him with amusements for days on end.

Wolfe, however, is immovable in a positive sense, a strength of character that outweighs his foibles and gives him appeal. Nero Wolfe is reliable. His associates, clients, and friends can count on him, for his dependability is like a massive rock, rivaling Wolfe's own bulk for stability. Inspector Cramer, the gruff but amiable police official who regularly contests cases with Wolfe, distrusts the detective's famed trickery. However, once Nero Wolfe gives his word, Cramer desists, because Wolfe's word is absolutely trustworthy. "What the tongue promises, the body must do," Wolfe once muttered to Archie, as he roused himself from rest to dress for a formal dinner he had committed himself to attend.

Nero Wolfe's reliability is refreshing at a time when faithfulness seems to be out of fashion, even among Christians. Faithfulness is hard because it goes against the grain of self-indulgence. Yet faithfulness is

74

a fruit of the Spirit we must cultivate if we are to be like Jesus.

JESUS, THE PATTERN

As he does for all the fruit of the Spirit, Jesus shows us what reliability is like better than anyone else. Jesus' faithfulness was grounded in his relationship with his Father. Jesus did everything the Father expected of him, exactly as he was supposed to. Scripture says Christ "was *faithful* to the one who appointed him" and that he "was faithful as a son, and as the master in the house" (Hebrews 3:2, 6 / JB).

As a boy of twelve, when Jesus' earthly parents found him among the teachers in the Temple, Jesus explained his three-day absence as a matter of duty. He asked Mary why they had been looking for him, pointing out that he had to take care of his Father's affairs (Luke 2:49). Even in an event that appeared superficially to be irresponsible, Jesus was being faithful. Later on he would explain to Jews who challenged him: "I can do nothing by myself; / . . . my aim is to do not my own will, / but the will of him who sent me" (John 5:29-30 / JB).

Jesus was perfectly reliable in his personal relationships. The people closest to him knew they could completely count on him. Martha and Mary, for example, believed that if Jesus had only been in Bethany, he would have kept Lazarus alive. "Martha said to Jesus, 'Lord, if you had been here, my brother would not have died. And even now I know that whatever you ask from God, God will give you' " (John 11:21 / RSV). In his final prayer before the crucifixion, Jesus tells the Father that he has finished the work he has been given to do. He says he has kept those given him true to God and none of them was lost, except Judas who chose to turn away (John 17:4-12).

Jesus' faithfulness reflected the Father's unqualified reliability, and ours should too. When God revealed his name to Moses, he said he was "faithful," which can be expressed as "worthy of confidence" (Exodus 34:6). The Lord is worthy of confidence, because he characteristically accomplishes what he promises to do. He said this about the effectiveness of his word: "Yes, as the rain and the snow come down from the heavens and do not return without watering the earth, making it yield and giving growth to provide seed for the sower and bread for the eating, so the word that goes from my mouth does not return to me empty, without carrying out my will and succeeding in what it was sent to do" (Isaiah 55:10-11 / JB). The Lord does what he says, and because of this faithfulness his people may lean the full weight of their lives on him with assurance. So our faith broadens into trust, expanding from the limits of intellectual assent to boundless reliance on God.[15]

MARKS OF FAITHFULNESS

Faithfulness, or reliability, has several distinctive features. Let's look more closely at three of them.

√ *A reliable person can be counted on to fulfill his or her responsibilities.* Jesus taught us about faithfulness in the context of speaking about his Second Coming. He chose two parables, one about the conscientious steward and another about the five wise bridesmaids. The master who returns to find his servant doing his job faithfully rewards him by placing him over the entire household (Matthew 24:45-51). The bridegroom who arrives unexpectedly greets the five bridesmaids who have responsibly kept their lamps trimmed and full of oil. They enter the wedding hall with him for the celebration (Matthew 25:1-13). Their counterparts were punished, the dishonest servant for his unfaithfulness and the five foolish bridesmaids for their irresponsibility.

When Mary Lou and I moved to Florida in 1985, we bought an older family home with many little things needing repair. Mary Lou will tell you that I am handy in the narrow sense of being right there, but that I am not very handy in the more important sense of being able to fix things. For more involved jobs, we have had to call on the services of handymen.

Recently we have had three experiences with repairmen, only one of whom deserves to be called reliable. I phoned the first three times, requesting that he repair a door, and while he agreed to consider the work, he never showed up. The second did shoddy work, leaving glue and plaster marks on wallpaper and breaking other things as a result of his work. The third came the day he was called to look at the work, completing the work the next day efficiently, neatly, and for a reasonable price. (Would you like his name and phone number?) We are supposed to be dependable in this down-to-earth sense in whatever the Lord has given us to do.

√ *A reliable person does more than the minimum.* I had the third handyman seal a leaky brick wall. While he was at work, he noticed a small hole in a cement block on the other side of the house, which he repaired

77

free of charge. We had not discussed that problem. He fixed it because it was a problem that he had noticed and that he could solve easily.

He is like the servants that the master praised and rewarded in the parable of the talents, which Jesus told immediately after the parables of the responsible steward and the five wise bridesmaids. The two servants who doubled their master's money by investing it could have satisfied his expectations minimally by banking it at interest. That's what he told the one who returned his money without any increment. "Then you ought to have invested my money with the bankers, and at my coming I should have received what was my own with interest" (Matthew 25:27 / RSV). However, the enterprising servants did even more than was required. Dependability is like that.

✓ *A reliable person's word is good.* A well-known administrator in a major Christian organization promised his two sons that he would play pool with them two Thursdays each month. The man treated that commitment seriously — he had given his boys his word. Once, an emergency board meeting involving some internationally famous leaders was called for a Thursday night. It was assumed that the staff could be there.

"I won't be able to be there," said the administrator. "That's the night I play pool with my sons."

It may have been assumed that for important people, he could reschedule his night with his boys. But they were important too, and he had made a commitment. Had he broken it, what would it have taught his sons (and the board members) about keeping one's word? The administrator kept his previous engagement with his boys, and the board meeting was rescheduled for a different evening.

Doing what you say you will do is God-like behavior, and it is one of the main ways that we are supposed to be like him.

LOYALTY

My candidate for the best fiction of the twentieth century is J.R.R. Tolkien's wonderful trilogy, *The Lord of the Rings*. Fiction is good if the author creates a world that has the feel of truth, and none feels truer to me than Tolkien's story. In this fantasy, a ring is found that has the power to bring all the world under the authority of Sauron, who is a minion of the devil. This ring was fashioned at the Mountain of Fire in Mordor, a land that was hell on earth. The ring could be destroyed only by returning it there.

A company of valiant creatures — men, elves, dwarfs, hobbits, and a wizard — is formed to undertake the secret mission of destroying the ring by throwing it back into the fire from whence it came. (Hobbits, incidentally, are humanoid beings, shorter and thicker than people; they are merry folks who enjoy the simple things of life, especially a lot of good food.)

I am not going to condense the three volumes here, but I want to focus on Frodo Baggins and Samwise ("Sam") Gamgee, two of the hobbits in the fellowship. Frodo and Sam are marked by excellent qualities, including love, humility, and faithfulness.

Because of his excellence, Frodo is chosen as the bearer of the ring and charged with casting it back into the Mountain of Fire, a mission he pursues doggedly across the land. Because he has given his word, nothing can stop this faithful hobbit from completing his task, not even the hellish gates of Mordor. At the outskirts of the wicked kingdom, with the imposing gates impassable, Sam thinks for a moment that the mission has ended in failure, but Frodo was determined:

" 'I am commanded to go to the land of Mordor, and therefore I shall go,' said Frodo. 'If there is only one way, then I must take it. What comes after must come.'

"Sam said nothing. The look on Frodo's face was enough for him; he knew that words of his were useless. And after all he never had any real hope in the affair from the beginning; but being a cheerful hobbit he had not needed hope, as long as despair could be postponed. Now they were come to the bitter end. But he had stuck to his master all the way; that was what he had chiefly come for, and he would still stick to him. His master would not go to Mordor alone. Sam would go with him. . . ."[16]

Sam was picked as part of the secret company because of his loyalty to Frodo. Frodo's mission would wear him down physically and spiritually, and the architects of the scheme knew he would need someone to stand by him. Sam foraged for food, nursed Frodo when he was sick, dragged or carried him when he was exhausted. His loyalty was a key factor in the completion of the mission.

Loyalty is faithfulness expressed in close personal relationships. Husbands and wives, parents and children, brothers and sisters, and close Christian friends should have this kind of faithfulness to one another. Loyalty is an outgrowth of Christian love. Paul says,

"Love bears all things, believes all things, hopes all things, endures all things" (1 Corinthians 13:7 / RSV).

For most of our adult lives, Mary Lou and I have had two or three friends who have stood with us and we with them. We confide in them, review major decisions with them, ask their advice on important family matters, and so on. If at all possible, everyone ought to have this kind of relationship with someone. However, many people have never formed close friendships. Others have lost them through divorce or some other tragic breakup. We find it hard to develop new loyalties when old ones did not work out. However, we must work at it, for we all need faithful friends to help us reach our destination. We each need a Sam Gamgee and should be a Sam Gamgee for a few others.

TRUSTFULNESS

Trustfulness is faithfulness pointed in the other direction, or more accurately, faithfulness pointed in the direction of another. We are trustful when we choose to rely on someone, whether that person has earned our trust or not.

When Jesus chose his disciples, he was careful to pick worthy men. He scrutinized candidates prayerfully and selected men he thought he could rely on. The Bible does not give details about the call of Judas Iscariot, but we can be sure that the Lord became aware that Judas would ultimately betray him. Yet Jesus trusted Judas. He put Judas in charge of finances for him and the disciples. Jesus kept him in that position, even though he knew Judas was taking money from the common fund (John 12:6). Jesus could see the good in this man, and he delighted in it. He also saw the evil, but hoped that his love of Judas would win him completely over. Jesus hoped that his trust of Judas would make him trustworthy.

Trustfulness has the power to strengthen others and to bring out their goodness. For example, when we lack confidence in a child, he may fail partly because he feels we don't trust him. We may never say a negative word, but our body language says it all for us. However, our expression of trust may be just the boost a child needs to do some generous deed or to resist a temptation.

We ought to take the example of Jesus, who trusted Judas, and be trustful of the people close to us. There may be some extreme cases where people are so unreliable that to trust them would be a threat to life or limb. Most of the time, however, we should trust others. We will find ourselves reaping a harvest of good.

INTEGRITY

John speaks of "doing what is true," and while the expression may strike us as sounding a bit odd, it conveys an important message. He is concerned with integrity, which is the correspondence of our words and our deeds. "But he who does what is true comes to the light, that it may be clearly seen that his deeds have been wrought in God" (John 3:21 / RSV).

There is a connection between truth and faithfulness. For example, Jesus always did what he said; his actions corresponded to his words. He proclaimed grace to the sinful and the sick, so he ate with sinners and healed the sick. Paul also brought together truth and faithfulness in his life and teaching. "We prove we are servants of God by great fortitude in times of suffering . . . by the word of truth" (2 Corinthians 6:4-7 / JB).

This integrity of word and deed is a form of faithfulness. If we live by the truth, John says, we will want our behavior to come to the light so that all can see how our actions conform to the truth. We will tolerate no discrepancy between what we believe and what we do, and so prove ourselves to be truly like Jesus.[17]

Humility: At Your Service 10

As Jesus' ministry was approaching its climax, his disciples were frequently distracted by thoughts of their importance. They argued among themselves about who was the greatest (Mark 9:34). James and John asked for high positions in his kingdom, which they expected Jesus to establish soon (Mark 10:37). Their view that places at the top were the places of importance, honor, and power is still commonly held.

The disciples had not yet understood that Jesus was setting a new standard, one that would — and did — turn the world upside down. He told them, "Blessed are the meek, for they shall inherit the earth" (Matthew 5:5 / RSV). In Jesus' kingdom, the important people are those who occupy the lowest place and serve all the others.

Once, when the disciples asked who was greatest in the kingdom, Jesus gave them an object lesson. He set a child in front of them and said, "Unless you change and become like little children you will never enter the kingdom of heaven. And so, the one who makes himself as little as this little child is the greatest in the kingdom of heaven" (Matthew 18:3-4 / JB).

People sometimes misinterpret this text to mean that Jesus set children as the standard for Christian maturity and told us to imitate them. Anyone who has spent some time with a few children knows firsthand how dubious this interpretation is. Some qualities of children (such as simplicity and trust) are worthy of imitation, but others are not. Children can be mean, rebellious, and selfish — all traits we would not want to copy. Jesus was pointing not to qualities of children, but to their place in society. "Become like little children" meant "place yourself in the position of children," who stand at the lowest place.

Jesus said this plainly when he settled the dispute over who was the greatest that erupted at the Last Supper: "Let the greatest among you become as the youngest, and the leader as one who serves" (Luke 22:26 / RSV). It was the child's place to serve everyone, and that's the place Jesus reserved for his followers.

HUMILITY, MEEKNESS, GENTLENESS

Humility, meekness, and gentleness are three words commonly used in the New Testament to name the character trait Jesus was describing here. However, for different reasons these words do not always communicate the concept well. Gentleness transmits the ideas of gracious behavior, of mildness, and of courtesy, which are part of the quality, but it does not clearly convey the central elements of lowliness and service.

Meekness and humility are good words for the virtue, but they have acquired connotations that conceal the Christian meaning. Of the two, meekness has the poorer image. The word is rare in everyday speech. It strikes us as quaint or old-fashioned. Meekness has been so drained of its strengths that it has become a fault. A meek person is thought to be passive, weak, indecisive, non-assertive — a milquetoast.

In contemporary usage, humility has come to refer to low self-esteem. For example, those who are shy or withdrawn, or socially insecure, or full of self-hatred, may be praised for their "humility." Given the impoverishment of meekness and the abuse of humility, what must people think Jesus meant when he described himself as "meek" and "humble of heart" (see Matthew 11:29)?

However, the word humility seems to carry enough of the true meaning to be useful. People still oppose humility to pride, which is correct. The word also continues to suggest an attitude of lowliness. I think we can rescue the word humility for Christian use. To reclaim the word we must stop using humility to refer to low self-esteem and we must restore the missing pieces to its meaning.

In the New Testament, humility translates as two Greek words, *prautes* and *tapeinophrosune*. These in turn represent words derived from Hebrew roots that mean poor, afflicted, weak, and humble. In this lineage, humility contains at its core two key qualities of the poor and lowly: absolute dependence on God and willingness to serve.

Throughout the Old and New Testaments, the poor were defenseless, without rights and oppressed; they had no one to come to their aid except God himself, and he did. When Mary celebrated the coming of the kingdom, she sang: "He has put down the mighty from their thrones, / and exalted those of lowly degree; / he has filled the hungry with good things, / and the rich he has sent empty away" (Luke 1:52-53 / RSV). Humble people rely on God to care for them and that dependence marks their character.

The ancient words for humility described the self-effacement and submission of the person who served someone else. Slaves were said to humble themselves in obedience to their masters. Humility is the disposition of one who serves, and in the New Testament it often means simply "willingness to serve." The great hymn that Paul cites to the Philippians goes straight to the heart of the matter. Paul wrote, "Have this mind among yourselves, which was in Christ Jesus, who, though he was in the form of God, did not count equality with God a thing to be grasped, but emptied himself, taking the form of a servant, being born in the likeness of men. And being found in human form he humbled himself and became obedient unto death, even death on a cross. Therefore God has highly exalted him" (Philippians 2:5-9 / RSV). Here the two core elements of humility converge in Jesus, who was willing to serve even to the point of offering himself in death and who depended entirely upon God for his life.[18]

The New Testament uses the root words for humility in contexts that round out our picture. These applications highlight particular qualities of a good servant.

✓ *Courtesy*. Paul instructed Titus to teach Christians to relate to everyone respectfully. "Remind them . . . to be gentle, and to show perfect courtesy toward all men" (Titus 3:1-2 / RSV). His motive, I think, is evangelistic, for the respectful behavior of Christians will intrigue neighbors enough to make them curious about its source.

✓ *Teachability*. A humble person is not fascinated with his own ideas and readily learns from instruction. James urges us to be teachable, to receive with meekness the word which has been planted in us and which can bring us to salvation (James 1:21).

✓ *Gentleness*. A humble person acts modestly and with restraint, especially in the face of opposition. Paul told Timothy that "a servant of the Lord is not to engage in quarrels, but has to be kind to everyone, a good teacher, and patient. He has to be gentle when he corrects people who dispute what he says, never forgetting that God may give them a change of mind so that they recognise the truth" (2 Timothy 2:24-25 / JB).

ANTIDOTE FOR ARROGANCE

Imagine that you are at a state banquet held in honor of the president of the United States. After supper, before giving his formal address, the president rises from his place, puts on a waiter's apron, and serves dessert and coffee to all of the guests. Such an event would shock us, but not nearly so much as Jesus' conduct stunned the disciples at the Last Supper. Jesus, who is the Lord, put on the work clothes of a slave and performed the duties of a slave by washing the disciples' feet. Peter's vigorous resistance registered their surprise. Jesus told his followers that he had given them an example so that they may copy what he had done to them (John 13:1-16). Here the Lord made humility the standard against which his disciples must measure themselves.

Something deep inside us reacts at the thought of performing for others so intimate a service as washing their feet. Feet are "dirty" and "smelly," and we don't like to handle them. We feel that there is something about washing others' feet that is beneath our dignity. It's that very something that Jesus is trying to get at by telling us to serve one another. Nothing makes us more unlike Jesus than pride, and the Lord prescribed humility as preventive medicine against that worst of spiritual diseases.

You don't have to survey the scene and declare yourself the greatest in order to be arrogant, although that would qualify you for the title. When pride is high and mighty it's easy to discern; its low and mighty variety is just as wicked and harder to see. The sense of self-importance that holds us at arm's length from others is arrogance in a smaller-size package. We hold ourselves aloof not because we think we're the best — we think we're just a little bit better.

Arrogance is always right. If you question it, it resists and may bristle with anger. Arrogance always gets its own way, pursuing its own wants and preferences. Arrogance cannot stand to be inconvenienced. It does not understand or accept explanations people give when they fail to keep a commitment. Arrogance is thoroughly self-reliant. It must be in control of even the smallest details, for it is sure that no one else can do things quite as well.

We may see something of ourselves in this pride's litany, for arrogance taints many of us. Among Christians, however, the people called to leadership are especially prone to it. Spiritual responsibility for others seems to carry in its baggage the temptation to self-importance. This was Jesus' concern as he worked to diffuse the disciples' interest in determining who was the greatest. The gravity of pride's threat evoked the Lord's severe warning: "He who is greatest among you shall be your servant; whoever exalts himself will be humbled, and whoever humbles himself will be exalted" (Matthew 23:11-12 / RSV). Then modeling the gentleness that is characteristic of humility, he made himself their example by serving them. Jesus asked the disciples, "For which is the greater, one who sits at table, or one who serves? Is it not the one who sits at table? But I am among you as one who serves" (Luke 22:27 / RSV).

Paul also pitted humility against pride. He said, "There must be no competition among you, no conceit; but everybody is to be self-effacing. Always consider the other person to be better than yourself, so that nobody thinks of his own interests first but everybody thinks of other people's interests instead" (Philippians 2:3-4 / JB). Paul is not telling us to maintain a constant mental picture of ourselves as being inferior to everybody else. That would be afflicting us with the emotional problem of low self-esteem, which, ironically, our humble service can help cure by giving us a sense that we're worth something to others. Paul is not speaking about our feeling inferior but about our position in relation to others. If we consider others "better" we are willing to serve them, to put their interests ahead of ours. That disposition makes us humble and drives arrogance away, for humility and arrogance are mutually exclusive and cannot occupy the same heart.

Not long ago I phoned the office of the large church I attend, and the voice at the other end of the line said, "Good morning, this is Paul Henry. How can I help you?" Since I had expected to make my request to the secretary, I was startled to have directly reached the pastor himself. I explained that I wanted to get a copy of an article he had quoted in his sermon the previous Sunday. He said he would be glad to dig it out, photocopy it, and send it to me.

This small, seemingly insignificant event impressed me. I remembered that when I first visited Orlando I had come across Paul Henry's name on a card in my motel room. It read: "If you have some need that you would like to discuss with a clergyman, please feel free to call Reverend Paul Henry at [such-and-such phone number]." At that time I thought that man must either have a servant's heart or a lot of time on his hands.

When I joined the parish, I soon learned that the latter — "a lot of time on his hands" — was not the case. Paul Henry is pastor of a church of nine thousand people, the largest congregation of any denomination in Florida; he leads a staff of thirty professionals; he supervises many ministries, organizations, and activities. He has every reason to be proud, for last year the American Catholic bishops consulted him and nine other pastors of successful large parishes to find out how they do it. Yet he has the time to care for visitors and to do small favors for parishioners. Sometimes he even answers the parish office phone. No room for arrogance here.

PRACTICAL HUMILITY

One night, not long after the Lord's resurrection, Peter followed his impulse to go fishing, and six other disciples joined him. They worked all night and caught nothing. Their limbs drooped with weariness and they were disappointed that they had caught no fish. After daybreak, when they approached the shore, a man shouted to them, "Have you caught anything, friends?"

"No!" they replied. It was Jesus, but they had not recognized him.

"Throw the net out to starboard," he said, "and you'll find something." So they dropped the net, and there were so many fish that they could not haul in their tremendous catch.

Then with a flash of recognition one of them said to Peter, "It is the Lord."

Peter threw a cloak about himself, jumped from the boat, and splashed the short distance to the shore. The rest followed in the boat, dragging the net behind.

When they reached land, Jesus asked them to bring some of the fish they had caught. There was bread there, and he was already broiling some fish over a charcoal fire. He invited the disciples to have breakfast, and he fed them as he had before on loaves and fishes. (Based on John 21:1-14 / JB.)

The simplicity and naturalness of this meeting of Jesus and his friends is striking. We might have expected the risen Lord to have been more supernatural, more ethereal. We might have imagined a more dramatic meeting, perhaps a cloud enveloping them in a throne room, the scent of heavenly perfume, the sound of music never heard before on earth. No. There was nothing but the down-to-earth smell of breakfast cooking and the sounds of the sea. Jesus met his friends as their servant, looking for ways of satisfying their simple human needs. He soothed their frustration by showing them where to find some fish. He knew they would be hungry after a long night's fishing, so he cooked them breakfast.

The Lord wanted to be sure that we did not take too spiritual an approach to humility, so he set a very practical example. Sometimes we pray for humility and then do nothing about it. Praying for the right dispositions of heart is laudable, but it is not enough. Humility comes to us in simple, worldly acts of serving others.

The Amazing Grace of Self-Control

11

March 9, 1748, was the turning point in the life of John Newton.[19] Up to that date, the twenty-two-year-old Newton had been a profligate. As a boy, Newton had been unruly and disobedient. His seafaring father first put him in a boarding school and then apprenticed him on a merchant ship. The youth was incorrigible and wild. Aboard ship Newton disregarded orders, picked fights with everyone, and because of his disruptive conduct he was dismissed.

Later he was impressed into the British Navy, but in 1745, at age twenty, he escaped. He was captured and punished as a deserter by being assigned to a ship engaged in the slave trade. With the female slaves available to the crew, John Newton gratified his sexual desires as much as he wanted. Remembering his youthful wildness, Newton said, "I believe for some years I never was an hour in any company without attempting to corrupt" such company.

Newton's life reached bottom on the African coast in Sierra Leone, where he had left the ship to work for a slave owner. The slaver's wife hated Newton, and when he got very sick, she withheld food and water and had her slaves torture him. He endured this maltreatment for more than a year.

Then came the series of events that turned John Newton's life around. His father had asked captains of slave ships to look for John, and in February, 1747, the ship *Greyhound* found him and took him aboard. On March 9, 1748, the pivotal day, to relieve his boredom, he picked up and read the great spiritual classic *The Imitation of Christ*. The book's warnings so upset Newton that he threw it aside. The next morning, a storm battered the *Greyhound,* caving in part of its side, and it appeared that the ship was doomed. Pumping seemed futile, but Newton and some others pumped for seven hours. John Newton did something more — he called on God to have mercy. From that time his life was never the same.

Newton did not change suddenly. However, as he drew closer to the Lord, he was gradually but radically transformed. He continued working in the slave trade, but his growing Christian spirit impelled him to be kind to the blacks. In 1754 a minor stroke ended his seafaring, and John Newton became tide surveyor for Liverpool, England. Here he entered his real career of Christian service. He studied the Bible, began to preach as a lay minister, and also started writing hymns. Responding to a call to the ministry, he served as a curate in a little village from 1764 until 1779 and then as a pastor in a distinguished London church. In that office, John Newton was a profound personal influence on the parliamentary leader William Wilberforce, persuading him to persevere in his political career and supporting his antislavery crusade.

However, John Newton is best known for his hymn "Amazing Grace," which is one of the most popular songs of all time. Newton put there a thumbnail sketch of his personal salvation. You are probably familiar with the first verse: "Amazing grace, how sweet the sound, that saved a wretch like me. I once was lost and now am found, . . ." John Newton's life fell into two unequal parts: twenty-two disoriented years peppered with debauchery and sixty years of steady and significant Christian service. The Lord's direct intervention was the dividing line.

Of all the pieces the Lord had to put into place for John Newton, I think the amazing grace that pulled everything else together was the fruit of the Spirit called self-control. The power of the Holy Spirit tamed Newton's wildness. Self-control subdued his passions. A dissipated life with no center became a life oriented around the Lord and around bringing others to him. Before grace broke in, John Newton's life read like the catalog of vices listed in Galatians 5:19 — fornication, impurity, licentiousness, and fighting. However, after grace struck, he developed self-control, which is both the response and the cure to these particular works of the flesh.

TAMING WILD DESIRES

We mainly think of self-control as the power to restrain sexual desires, and that is a big part of it. In the course of setting a high moral standard for his disciples, Jesus said: "Every one who looks at a woman lustfully has already committed adultery with her in his heart. If your right eye causes you to sin, pluck it out and throw it away; it is better that you lose one of your members than that your whole body be thrown into hell. And if your right hand causes you to sin, cut it off and throw it away; it is better that you lose one of your members than that your whole body go into hell" (Matthew 5:27-30 / RSV). Jesus' hard advice proves how few biblical literalists there really are. Many Christians must fight strong sexual temptations, but how many have you met who have dealt with them by plucking out their eye or removing their hand? I don't think Jesus was giving us a command that he expected us to take literally. He was using hyperbole to show how serious he is about our controlling ourselves.

The teaching of Jesus on self-control applies to other troublesome areas. We are subject to a set of passions that have the strength to dominate our lives. For example, a single-minded envy or greed or hatred has consumed many a person. Strong feelings such as anger or fear will also control us unless we curb them.

The purpose of self-control is to put us in charge of our actions, to prevent our bodies from committing sin. However, self-control's main field of operation is internal. Wild desires and unruly feelings work in our minds. They plant seeds in our thoughts that bear fruit in evil deeds. For example, we may meditate enviously on the gifts and accomplishments of others. Before long a huge, ugly envy tree has rooted itself in our personal landscape and it drops its foul fruit everywhere. We can't stand to be with such gifted or successful individuals, so we snub them; we can't resist speaking against them to our friends, and we find other snappy ways to injure them.

Jesus exhorted us to stop committing adultery in our thoughts, and it is in our minds that self-control must work to discipline all of our desires and feelings. We cannot stop tempting thoughts from popping up, but we do not have to invite them to hang around. When we begin to envy someone, for example, we can change the topic of our mind's conversation. The sooner we drop the subject and take up another the more effective we'll be in resisting the sin.

The mind is also the primary arena where we choose to break addictions and to establish control over drunkenness and dependence on drugs. Physical and chemical factors complicate the process of getting free from substance abuse. Some professional help is almost always necessary to assist in doing the job. However, self-control is the enforcer of decisions to stop drinking or using drugs. For example, Alcoholics Anonymous recognizes that persons prone to drunkenness must maintain their sobriety by disciplining their thoughts. Thus they must always honestly face their problem and acknowledge their reliance on the power of God and the support of others. Successful programs that deal with other addictions likewise base maintaining freedom from the problem on self-control.

MORE THAN SELF-MASTERY

There is a well-established tradition in our culture that places a high value on self-control. Ancient philosophers, like Plato and Aristotle, esteemed it as a way of restraining sensual desires in order to contribute to human happiness. The school of Stoic philosophy taught that we could be happy only if we exercised enough self-control to sample some things in moderation and to avoid some things altogether. They believed they could prevent unhappiness by disciplining themselves not to react badly to circumstances. You will find versions of these approaches to self-control persisting in contemporary self-help programs. Many Christians adopt this classic idea of self-mastery, thinking mistakenly that they are avidly pursuing the Christian quality.

However, Christian self-control differs from classic self-mastery on two key points:

✓ *Self-control is empowered by the Holy Spirit*, while classic self-mastery is exclusively dependent upon willpower. True, Christian self-control also involves the will. However, we do not achieve freedom from dominating passions by acting on our own but by engaging the power of the Holy Spirit to reinforce the decisions of our will. Our wills alone do not have the strength to master forces like lust or anger. Subduing them depends upon the action of the Spirit. His presence makes self-control qualitatively different from classic self-mastery.

✓ *Self-control and classic self-mastery have different purposes.* The latter aims for autonomy, to put people fully in control of their own destiny. However, self-control does not seek to put us in charge of our ultimate direction and it does not authorize us to shape our lives as we please. The purpose of self-control is to free us from domination by desires, feelings, and addictions so that we can fashion our lives as God desires.

We should be sure that we are not settling for something less than real self-control.

DISCIPLINE

Self-control has another important dimension that Scripture presents as related to the discipline of athletic training. Paul says: "Do you not know that in a race all the runners compete, but only one receives the prize? So run that you may obtain it. Every athlete exercises self-control in all things. They do it to receive a perishable wreath, but we an imperishable. Well, I do not run aimlessly, I do not box as one beating the air; but I pommel my body and subdue it, lest after preaching to others I myself should be disqualified" (1 Corinthians 9:24-27 / RSV). Like athletes, who build strength and stamina for their contests, Christians must exercise repeated acts of self-control to prepare to finish their race, to maintain lifelong fidelity to Christ.

For the past year or so I have done my physical and spiritual exercises first thing in the morning. Each day before I start my aerobics, a little voice, which I envision as belonging to a very sluggish, laid-back part of me, says enticingly, "Let's skip it today. You don't really feel like it. Once won't hurt." I think the same inertia also prompts me to let slide my prayer and Scripture study. However, I know that if I don't continue to do regular physical exercise, I may not continue to enjoy good health. I am even more certain that without regular personal worship and Bible study, my Christian life will grow weak.

Persistence in Christian living depends upon a daily exercise of self-control in an even broader sense. I must have the freedom to respond to circumstances in a Christian manner, and the training ground for that is the daily discipline of conforming my life to God's will. By repeated acts of self-control I acquire the experience I will need to deal with unexpected situations.

In 4 Maccabees, a book found in some ancient Bible

manuscripts which, however, never has been regarded as canonical, we read about the Jewish philosopher Eleazar. He was a ninety-year-old leader who had trained himself to finish the race. The emperor Antiochus Epiphanes was punishing Jerusalem by forcing all the Jews to break their law by eating pork and meat sacrificed to idols.

Antiochus urged Eleazar to be reasonable, expecting God to understand that he would have been acting under compulsion. Eleazar believed that obedience to the law was a greater compulsion and he refused, even though he knew it meant torture and death. He said: "You scoff at our philosophy as though living by it were irrational, but it teaches us self-control, so that we master all pleasures and desires, and it also trains us in courage, so that we endure any suffering willingly; . . . I will not play false to you, O law that trained me, nor will I renounce you, beloved self-control" (4 Maccabees 5:22-23, 34 / RSV).[20]

All Christians must aspire to persevere, to remain faithful until the Lord finally claims them in death. For most of us, finishing the race will not mean martyrdom as it did for Eleazar, although for some it may. However, all of us will meet evils that will test our mettle.

How will we handle frustration and failure? Will financial problems turn us away from God? How will we react to the untimely death of a loved one? Will we finally give in to a temptation we have fought for years? We can all expect daily battles that can rob us of our life in the Spirit. We can also count on the amazing grace of self-control to get us ready to fight them.

Isaiah said that God would be with the Messiah to help him withstand opposition, and he foretold accurately that Jesus would "set [his] face like flint," knowing that God would see him through (Isaiah 50:7 / JB). So the pattern for our self-control is Jesus himself, who moved through his life confidently facing whatever came. Consider the following examples:

√ Jesus was subject to strong emotions, but he never lost control. Even his most forceful expression of anger, when he chased people and animals from the Temple (John 2:13-22), was deliberate and controlled. He chose to get angry; he took the time to fashion a whip out of cord; and he used his feeling to accomplish his goal of cleansing his Father's house.

√ Jesus faced opposition calmly and walked through it without letting it deflect his purpose. For example, when the Jews challenged him for curing a sick man on the sabbath, he said: "You study the scriptures, / believing that in them you have eternal life; / now these same scriptures testify to me, / and yet you refuse to come to me for life! / As for human approval, this means nothing to me" (John 5:39-41 / JB). Unruffled, he continued on his course.

√ Jesus maintained his balance even when his ministry was rocked by failures. For example, many followers abandoned him over his teaching that he was the living bread (John 6:51, 59-66). Though he must have been frustrated and disappointed, he did not lose his equanimity.

√ As the shadow of the cross fell imminently across

his path and death drew near, Jesus felt mortal fear. Mark records that Jesus took Peter, James, and John with him to Gethsemane, "And he . . . began to be greatly distressed and troubled. And he said to them, 'My soul is very sorrowful, even to death' " (Mark 14:33-34 / RSV). He struggled visibly with this emotion, but grace and his self-control saw him through the test.

✓ For three years Jesus walked calmly toward the climax of his life. As the final sequence of events engulfed him, he endured them with steadfastness. A life of self-control had done its work, and he was ready. Nothing distracted him from his purpose — not betrayal, humiliation, scourging, mockery, the crowning with thorns, injustice, rejection, exhaustion, crucifixion, or excruciating pain.

Painful circumstances will also crash in on us, pressuring us to depart from our course. We can be sure of it. However, the amazing grace of self-control will help us pass through them calmly and confidently. John Newton put it in a nutshell in his song: "Through many dangers, toils and snares, we have already come. 'Twas grace that brought us safe thus far and grace will lead us home."

PART TWO

*How We Become
More Like
Jesus*

The Water Is for the Flowers

12

It is easy to motivate people to want Christ's character traits. Even opponents of Christianity admire Jesus and want in some ways to be like him. However, the sticking point is how to get them. We know what we are like. Who is more in touch than we with our mean streaks, our irritability, or our impatience? We believe that the Lord wants to change us, repairing our broken likeness to conform to his. But how does it come about? What must we do to become more like Christ? How do we begin to grow in love, joy, peace, patience, and kindness?

The first answer to these questions is that we cannot do anything to produce the fruit of the Spirit for ourselves, because our transformation in Christ is God's work. The second answer, however, is that we must do everything we can to cooperate with the Lord in the process. While we cannot make ourselves more like Christ, the more we understand how we grow spiritually, the more readily we can advance to Christian maturity. In the following chapters we will look at ways we acquire the fruit of the Spirit. First, we will focus in Chapters 12 through 14 on the Holy Spirit's work. Then in Chapters 15 through 17 we will look at our role of cooperating with grace.

Once, a teenager of mine experienced a rare inspiration, and decided to help his mother without being asked. He watered a silk-flower arrangement, which had been a gift from her mother.

As water trickled over the coffee table and splashed to the floor, he said sheepishly, "Oh. I guess you don't water these, do you?"

"No, son," said Mary Lou with a laugh. "The water is for the flowers, but not for these."

No amount of water could give life to that flower arrangement; nothing from within could animate it, or change it, or make it grow. For a garden of living plants, however, water is the lifeblood that accounts for sustenance and growth.

Theresa of Ávila, the great sixteenth-century woman of prayer, used watering a garden as an analogy to teach about life in the Holy Spirit. She said that as we progress in Christian living, we go through stages that parallel drawing water for a garden. When we start out our spiritual life, it is comparable to taking water from a well with a bucket or a pump. We must invest a great amount of labor to get a small amount of water. However, as God takes more initiative, our spiritual life becomes like a flowing stream or a torrential downpour.[21]

"The water is for the flowers," Theresa said, whether it comes by hard work or in torrents. Water nurtures myriads of plants in the garden. Without it the plants cannot live or grow. The same is true for us. The Holy Spirit is the source of our Christian life. His energy causes our sustenance and growth. He brings forth and nurtures the fruit of the Spirit in us. Just as watering the garden produces daisies, roses, and all kinds of beautiful flowers, the life of the Spirit in us produces love, peace, and all the characteristics of Jesus.

Theresa grounded her analogy on the teaching of Jesus, who compared the spiritual life to a rush of waters. He told the Samaritan woman that anyone who drank the water he would give would never be thirsty again. Jesus said, "Whoever drinks of the water that I shall give him will never thirst; the water that I shall give him will become in him a spring of water welling up to eternal life" (John 4:14 / RSV).

Shortly after this, at the Feast of Tabernacles in Jerusalem, Jesus declared to the crowds: "If any one thirst, let him come to me and drink. He who believes in me, as the scripture has said, 'Out of his heart shall flow rivers of living water' " (John 7:37-38 / RSV). Jesus was speaking vividly about the activity of the Holy Spirit.

The water analogy is instructive about the balance between God's role and our role in spiritual growth. It shows that we cannot do much to help the process. Our cooperation with grace is important, but if we tried to claim too big a role in producing the fruit of the Spirit, we would be making a mountain out of a molehill. The gardener can churn the ground with a spade, pull some weeds, put in some stakes, and so on. He works long and hard, but the sum of all his labor gives no life or growth at all to the flowers. Our effort accounts about as much for our spiritual growth. This does not mean that we should stop trying to be like Christ. It means we must stop trying to do it on our own, and let the Holy Spirit work in us.

109

THE VINE AND THE BRANCHES

We become like Christ because we are rooted in him and because the Holy Spirit is at work in us. If you think I am belaboring this point, you are right. We pay lip service to the truth that the Holy Spirit animates, inspires, directs, and shapes us; then we go off and behave as if we never heard of him.

Jesus paid considerable attention to this subject at the Last Supper in the important discourse that summed up his teaching. He said, "Abide in me, and I in you. As the branch cannot bear fruit by itself, unless it abides in the vine, neither can you, unless you abide in me. I am the vine, you are the branches. He who abides in me, and I in him, he it is that bears much fruit, for apart from me you can do nothing" (John 15:4-5 / RSV).

The analogy of the vine and the branches is an excellent image of Christian growth. A plant produces only fruit that is appropriate to it. We would be unpleasantly surprised to find onions growing on our strawberry plants, or brussels sprouts on our grapevines. Jesus is the vine; if we remain in him, we will bear his fruit. Therefore, we can expect to produce love, peace, goodness, humility, and all the traits that belong to Christ.

Branches that are broken from the vine cannot bear any fruit. Only branches that are united to the vine can be fruitful, since it is the life that courses through the plant which produces fruit. If we are to become more like Christ, bearing the same fruit he did, we must let the Holy Spirit work in us.

The Holy Spirit changes us without our having to

pay much attention to what he is doing. That's one of the messages Jesus conveyed by the vine analogy. A strawberry plant does not have to concentrate on producing strawberries — it doesn't have to master the definition of a strawberry; it doesn't have to observe how other strawberry plants do it; it doesn't have to tighten and exert its plant muscles. The life of the strawberry plant produces strawberries naturally. Similarly, our transformation in Christ advances without our having to think very much about it.

The story of Josephine, my Italian-American mother, is instructive here. Mother was a Catholic, a woman of great simple faith. She did many things well, but getting angry was one thing she did badly. She had to struggle with repressed anger, irritability, and even occasional outbursts. My mother resented it profoundly that both of her daughters left home when they turned twenty to pursue their careers. Her anger flared up now and then, adding tension to already strained relationships.

Mother's body was racked with cancer for a year before she died. Shortly after the diagnosis, she, along with all of her children, prayed that the Holy Spirit would work anew in her life. She also received the sacrament of the anointing of the sick, and all of us hoped she would be healed.

A marvelous thing happened. The cancer raged on, but the anger that gnawed at her was completely cured. A lady who for years had been angry just below the surface became fundamentally peaceful. No one had to counsel her. There was no self-help program or psychotherapy. Mother did not have to work hard at it, although she did have to tell my sisters she was sorry. She became more like Christ by the intervention of the Holy Spirit. She was reconciled to her daughters and spent several happy months with them before she died.

Like strawberries on a strawberry plant, that's how our spiritual growth comes. The Holy Spirit does it. Naturally. The main way we develop the fruit of the Spirit is by the direct action of God.

The Apple Does Not Fall Far from the Tree

13

"Insanity is hereditary," someone once observed. "Parents get it from their children." That's about the only thing that goes in that direction. In addition to their genetic inheritance, our children pick up many of our behavior patterns, mannerisms, and quirks.

I remember seeing a friend at a lecture, hunched over in his chair, looking pensive, with his chin resting on his fist. I chuckled as I noticed his seven-year-old son, sitting just behind him, hunched over in his chair, looking pensive, with his chin resting on his fist. Once, I overheard some teenaged girls discussing my oldest son. "Oh, talking to John Ghezzi is just like talking to his dad," said one of the girls. I took it as a compliment, though I doubt it was. As the old Slovenian saying goes, "The apple does not fall far from the tree."

Our children acquire our traits unconsciously. They become like us simply by being with us. If for some reason young children live with other adults for a long time, they assume their personal qualities. In the movie *The Emerald Forest*, which is based on a true story, a primitive South American tribe snatches a ten-year-old American boy from his parents. A decade later, the lad is thoroughly transformed in the image of his new family, and cannot be expected to return to his previous circumstances. He changed because he was removed from his parents to live with new — and very different — surrogate parents.

It is sad but true, children indiscriminately pick up the traits of their parents. Because fathers are sometimes bad, children get the bad with the good, manifesting the faults of their parents as well as their virtues. For example, I am intense, impulsive, and easily provoked to anger. These qualities have infected most of my children. Even those who appear to be somewhat carefree have their bouts with intensity and impulsive behavior. All seem to have caught my anger problem, which I probably "inherited" from my mother.

IN GOD'S PRESENCE

Just as children become like their parents by being around them, we become more like the Lord simply by being in his presence. The fruit of the Spirit are principles of action that manifest themselves in our conduct. However, the interior changes that enable us to act in contradiction to our strong, evil inclinations come from our nearness to God. Paul says that as we come before the Lord we "are being changed into his likeness from one degree of glory to another; for this comes from the Lord who is the Spirit" (2 Corinthians 3:18 / RSV).

Our transformation in the image of God occurs similarly to our transformation in the image of our parents. We are changed by our being in God's presence and not chiefly by our striving to be like him. There is a difference, however, between the way we acquire the fruit of the Spirit and the way we pick up our parents' traits.

114

Our acculturation in our families occurs without our having to pay attention to it. When we are growing up at home, we don't have to do anything to be with our mother or our father. Normally, we are around them enough to be molded in their likeness. But to become more like God, we must take some steps to be in his presence.

God is present everywhere, but it is not his omnipresence that makes us his replicas. To become more like the Lord, we must come into his presence in another, more personal sense. This illustration makes the point clearly. If I am reading in the family room, ensconced in my easy chair, and Clare, my nine-year-old daughter, enters the room, we are *present* in the same room, but we are not immediately *present* to one another. When she crawls up into my lap and gives me a hug, she engages me personally. We are now in each other's presence. As I set my book aside and speak with Clare, we communicate. I can affect her, and she can affect me.

Our becoming more like the Lord involves our coming into his presence in this way. We must engage him personally. This intimate communication between God and us is the activity of prayer. When we approach him in worship, we can touch him, and more importantly he can touch us.

There is a proportionality between time spent in prayer and the extent of our Christ-likeness. We can see this exemplified in the lives of great Christians throughout history. Francis of Assisi, for example, was so like Jesus that he has been called the "Christ" of the thirteenth century. Francis was so free of self-indulgence that he rejoiced in humiliation and suffering because Jesus suffered and was humiliated. What explains his resemblance to Jesus? His spending much time in prayer. He was constantly uniting himself with God.

This was also the case with Thomas More, who was chancellor of England under King Henry VIII, and with Brother Lawrence, the seventeenth-century monk who worked in the kitchen and wrote wisely about prayer. Thomas More was like Jesus in his generous love, his joyfulness, and his courage in the face of death, which came because he held to his convictions. He was one of the most famous leaders in his country, second in command to the king. Yet throughout his life Thomas More spent every Friday in prayer, reflecting on the crucifixion, death, and resurrection of his Lord.

Brother Lawrence says of himself that he was joyful and peaceful in all things, and everyone who met this humble kitchen helper recognized his closeness to God. Brother Lawrence radiated Christ. Why? He prayed throughout the day, as continuously as he was able. He did everything — even the smallest act, such as picking up a spoon he had dropped — for the love of God.

When we pray, loving God must be our focus, not concern for our spiritual growth. We will not produce more fruit of the Spirit if we consume our prayer time deciding how we are going to change. The more we fuss about our own agenda for personal growth, the more we may interfere with our own transformation. We may be like the gardener who keeps digging up his seeds to see if they have begun to grow.

Paul exhorts us in these words: "I appeal to you therefore, brethren, by the mercies of God, to present your bodies as a living sacrifice, holy and acceptable to God, which is your spiritual worship" (Romans 12:1 /

RSV). Our worship is to present ourselves to God as living sacrifices. What do the words "living sacrifice" call to your mind? I think of the sacrifice of animals in the Old Testament, whose blood was drained and poured out over the altar. And I think of the sacrifice of Jesus on the cross, pouring out his blood to atone for my sins. In both cases, the pouring out of blood meant the pouring out of a life as an offering to the Lord.

We are supposed to worship God in the same spirit, offering ourselves as a living sacrifice — as a living "pouring out of life." There is no place here for prayer that focuses on self. All attention is rightly placed on God. We change the most through prayer like this. In our total self-giving we resemble Christ more than at any other moment, and as God accepts our gift, he imprints his likeness in us more clearly.

I learned this principle about seventeen years ago from Reverend Graham Pulkingham, who at that time was rector of the Episcopal Church of the Redeemer in Houston, Texas. I was going through a time of personal stress due mainly to my being overextended. Like many Christian workers, I was trying to be all things to all men all by myself. One Sunday afternoon, I heard Graham speak about worshiping as a living sacrifice, and I responded immediately. The next morning I went to a quiet place to pray for about an hour. I spent my time worshiping God, giving myself to him, loving him. I meditated on the death and resurrection of Jesus. I prayed the Psalms, exalting God and celebrating his goodness. I went to the same place and worshiped the next day, and the next, and every workday after that. As that year slipped by, I noticed peace welling up in

117

me, displacing the anxiety pressure had caused. The growing sense of calm inspired me to take inventory of my commitments; I eliminated half of them, which restored a measure of sanity to my life. The change, however, came mainly from God as I gave myself to him in worship.

The fruit of the Spirit is a by-product of our prayer. How will we be able to tell when we have changed? When we have matured a little in love, generosity, or kindness? We probably won't notice, and that's the way it should be. We can't see our resemblance to the Lord very well, just as children don't seem to notice how much they are like their parents, until someone points it out. We should not be concerned about it. Jesus intended that others who did not yet know him would notice. He said, "By this all men will know that you are my disciples, if you have love for one another" (John 13:35 / RSV). Renewing us in God's image is primarily the Holy Spirit's work. If we spend time worshiping God faithfully and regularly, the apple will not fall far from the tree.

The Promise of Problems   14

In my Christian life, there has never been a time that was problem-free. There have only been good periods when I handled problems well, and bad periods when the problems handled me. Your experience may have been similar. Problems never seem nice when we have them, nor are they pleasant to go through. But as one of my friends says, "Problems are opportunities in working clothes." God acts through them to renew us in the likeness of Christ.

The Lord told us that we would have difficulties, so we ought to expect problems as a normal part of Christian living. I have always thought that those inspiring collections of Bible promises were misleadingly incomplete. Somewhere in your home, on a kitchen counter or at your desk, you may have a little book or a "promise box" with a daily verse offering something good from God — victory, deliverance, blessing, wealth. Such a "promise box" never seems to carry the Lord's promise of trials or troubles. Have you ever seen this verse in a collection of scriptural promises: "A servant is not greater than his master. / If they persecuted me, / they will persecute you too" (John 15:20 / JB)? Troubles hold a prominent place among the blessings the Lord promised those who follow him (Mark 10:30). A correct view of problems sees them as promised and promising.

How can anything so dangerous be promising? Problems can be our undoing, stripping us of faith and threatening our relationship with God. They are potentially fatal. Paradoxically, however, problems can be of great spiritual benefit. Difficulties that could sap all vitality from our Christianity can be occasions for vibrant new life in the Spirit. Trials that seem to be driving us away from God can ultimately draw us nearer to him.

This is the promise of problems: they are chances for us to become more like Christ. God puts us on the spot so that he can get at precisely those areas which make us most unlike his Son. As we face the difficulty with God's help, the fruit of the Spirit begins to replace the opposite weakness.

Take compassion and forbearance, for example. My world is chock-full of eccentric, irregular people who tend to rub me the wrong way. Some of the same kind of people probably intersect with you too. I just don't like the way they talk or the way they do things. If the truth be told, I don't like them very much. If I could avoid them, all would be well. But Jesus' commandment to love one another makes that escape impossible.

Every day I have a choice. Irregular people can be a problem for me, perhaps even an occasion for sin. For example, I can surround my personal space with an alarm system of selective irritability. I can choose to be nice only to people I like. People I don't like either get the message and keep their distance, or they get snubbed, ignored, or put down.

However, relating to people I don't like can be an occasion for growth in compassion and forbearance. Jesus' command to love others as he loved us (John 15:12) did not stipulate that we should serve only those people we happen to like. Jesus knew this would not be easy, but he sent the Holy Spirit to help us. I can count on grace to support me in being kind to those disagreeable, irritating people I meet at work, at the supermarket, at school, at church, and in the neighborhood. Maybe even in my own home. My problems with loving others can precipitate my growth in Christian qualities. Without the dynamic tension that comes from our difficulties, I doubt we would acquire much fruit of the Spirit at all.

THE VINEDRESSER

The Lord said that Christians could expect suffering, but he does not send us evil (James 1:13). Much of our pain is self-induced, a by-product of our evil desires as they develop into sins. However, while God does not cause our problems, he does permit them. He finds them useful in persuading us to open up to his grace. If we had no difficulties, we might go about our life imagining that we have everything under control, like little gods who see no need for God. The Lord mercifully allows us to have problems that make us face reality. When we finally turn to him, we will agree that the pain was worth it.

God takes some initiatives that cause us pain, and we may perceive his actions as problems. Jesus said, "I am the true vine, and my Father is the vinedresser. Every branch of mine that bears no fruit, he takes away, and every branch that does bear fruit he prunes, that it may bear more fruit" (John 15:1-2 / RSV). The Lord may ask us to give something we had expected to keep. That would be a problem, wouldn't it? Or we may have a difficulty when the Lord says no to something we want. Suppose a parent, spouse, or child contracts a fatal illness, and after every medical and spiritual route is explored, it becomes clear that this is his or her time to die. The Lord may want us to let go of our attachment to the person as part of our pruning, of our being shaped in the image of Christ. Yes, it hurts. But if we hold on to our anger, if we fight the Lord, if we withdraw from him in bitterness — the pain will be even worse.

When the Lord prunes us, he may be striking at a self-indulgent tendency or trimming back a personal preference, either of which may be obstructing our growth. However, like the vinedresser who cuts away healthy growth on his vines, the Lord sometimes prunes us simply to make us more fruitful.

When I first moved to Ann Arbor, Michigan, I bought a home with grapevines, raspberries, and fruit trees in the garden. The previous owner had not tended to the vines and trees, but they still bore some fruit. The harvest that first year was meager. The following spring, a young friend volunteered to help with yard work, which I welcomed. To my horror, he viciously chopped back the grapevines, raspberry bushes, and fruit trees, or so I thought. However, when harvesttime came in the next two years, the vines hung heavy with grapes, a far more plentiful supply than I thought possible. We had bushes bent over with raspberries, and our little peach trees overachieved in productivity. My friend had cut away dead wood and some healthy limbs, both in the interest of fruitfulness. God, our vinedresser, does the same to us. The result is that we bear more fruit of the Spirit.

Parents have an innate desire for their children to turn out all right. Minimally, they want them to grow up to be responsible people, adults who can survive everyday challenges. Usually, they expect more, hoping that their children will excel in some way and that they will develop good character traits. Mothers and fathers take steps to assure the end result they want. They train their children in specific behavior patterns so that the desired conduct becomes second nature to them. A mother, for example, who wants a teenaged son to be responsible may require him to work and pay for his own clothing.

Scripture says that God, our Father, relates to us just as parents do to their children. He wants us to become replicas of his Son, Jesus, so he works to sharpen our likeness to Christ. Thus, the Letter to the Hebrews explains that God trains us in order to produce the fruit of the Spirit in our lives: "Our human fathers were thinking of this short life when they punished us, and could only do what they thought best; but he does it all for our own good, so that we may share his own holiness. Of course, any punishment is most painful at the time, and far from pleasant; but later, in those on whom it has been used, it bears fruit in peace and goodness" (Hebrews 12:10-12 / JB).

Discipline is the business end of training. When it is on target, it hits the trainee where he is most vulnerable, the place where he must change or grow. However painful and unpleasant, discipline is the key to shaping the desired character trait.

For example, Mary Lou and I want our seven children to be good people, unselfish, marked with courage, hope, and the capacity to love, and we think smart discipline is one means to that end. So we frequently say no to a child's desire. While we would like our children to take no like yes, no always hurts. We also discipline our kids by setting limits, such as no television viewing until homework is done.

Our most unpopular rule illustrates well the connection between discipline and character formation. We have a driving age limit for family members: no child may drive a family car until he or she is seventeen years old, which is a full year beyond Florida's minimum age required for a driver's license. Now if you think that policy does not build character, just talk to one of our kids as he or she approaches age sixteen!

The rule tells our children in language they understand that driving is a privilege, not a right. Waiting a year prepares them to take seriously the responsibility of a driver for the safety of passengers and the vehicle. Most important, it takes a deep cut at self-indulgence, helping prepare the way for a life of unselfishness and charity.

We believe our children should have at least one distinction that sets them somewhat apart from their peers. Goodness will ultimately require them to turn their backs on what some others are doing. Our kids deserve a chance to practice breaking ranks, so Mary Lou and I give them this one.

My homey examples are puny when contrasted with what God's discipline does for us. Parents can train their children so that they will behave a little better. We can get them to be somewhat more selfless, perhaps a little more patient and kind. God's discipline, however, operates on a scale no mere human father or mother could approximate. He changes us, deep down, in ways moms and dads never could.

THE SWORDSMITH'S ART

God's discipline causes deeper pain too. If his punishment feels like fire, it is because he is forging the image of Christ in us, and fire is required to make us malleable. For this reason, God's training of us through our problems has been compared to the art of swordmaking.[22]

Japanese handmade swords are reputed to be the best in the world, unsurpassed in strength and flexibility. After selecting an iron bar, the swordsmith repeatedly heats it and hammers it out in order to drive out impurities and eliminate flaws that could cause crumbling. Then he hammers the bar to twice its length, folds it over, and hammers it out again. He repeats this process over and over, each time doubling the number of layers and bonding them until the resulting sword contains thousands of layers. This is the secret of the Japanese sword's extraordinary strength and flexibility.

Have you any empathy for that iron bar? I do. Anyone who has gone through a trial can easily see God as the swordsmith and oneself as the piece of iron. The Lord seems to heat up our life and hammer us out, eliminating impurities and flaws that come to the surface. Nothing like a problem to bring into the open various shortcomings such as anger, impatience, and pride, so that God can get at the root problem.

Just when we think the problem is over, he puts us through the fire again. (In case you missed the force of the last sentence, you might want to read it again, moving your lips.) Then he hammers and folds, hammers and folds, as he transforms us into replicas of Jesus. I remember once going through a severe depression due to personal failures, family difficulties, and a long-standing problem with overcommitment. After many hammerings and foldings, my life calmed and I felt stronger. One day as I was celebrating the end of this particular trial, I thanked God that I could get on with life without having to go through anything like that again. Then a thought came, like a thunderclap, and I'm sure it was from God. "Oh, no, Bert. Now that you have endured this trial you are strong enough to face even harder tests." And I have, each time knowing when the process started that I would be stronger and better when I came out at the other end.

The final step in forging the sword is tempering the edge, which the swordmaker accomplishes by heating the metal and quickly cooling it in water. This toughens the blade so that it will neither chip nor grow dull. The procedure requires great care, since too much heat will burn the metal, causing brittleness, while too little heat will result in softness that cannot hold an edge. We can be confident that God, who tempers us with trials, will not test us beyond our ability to endure (1 Corinthians 10:13). He does not want us to burn out or become fragile with brittleness. But we can count on him to give us enough heat so that we are not softened and blunted by every difficulty.

In the last three chapters we considered three

aspects of God's work in us to make us more like Christ:

- *The Water Is for the Flowers* — The Holy Spirit is the principle of new life in us who transforms us from within into replicas of Jesus.
- *The Apple Does Not Fall Far from the Tree* — We grow in the fruit of the Spirit by spending time in God's presence.
- *The Promise of Problems* — Problems can occasion our becoming more Christ-like by allowing the Lord to expose our weaknesses and replace them with his strengths.

God's work is certainly the most important part of the process. However, God cannot remake us in the image of his Son without our cooperation. It might be easier if he could, but he cannot do so without taking back the gift of free will that he has given us. And if we were merely passive recipients without the ability to respond to him freely, we would not be like Jesus. In the final three chapters we will look at various aspects of our free cooperation with God's grace so that our lives cannot help but produce the fruit of the Holy Spirit.

Do Whatever He Tells You 15

One day, Ananias, a faithful Jew and a follower of Jesus, was minding his own business as he went through his daily routine. If someone had told him that the Lord was about to direct him to get involved in an event that would affect the course of history, he would probably have chuckled, "Who, me? Not a chance, I'm just an ordinary man, not an important person."

We are not told at what time of day the Lord appeared to Ananias, but it was likely at a regular prayer time, possibly in the morning. His prayer was interrupted by a visitation from the Lord.

He heard the Lord say, "Ananias!" Luke tells us that Ananias had a vision in which the Lord spoke to him, so we can guess that the voice was not audible. But Ananias knew that the person addressing him was the Lord Jesus.

"Here I am, Lord," replied Ananias. Had he anticipated what was coming, Ananias might have feigned spiritual deafness.

"Ananias, you must go to Straight Street and ask at the house of Judas for someone called Saul, who comes from Tarsus."

Fear gripped Ananias as the Lord spoke. He had heard about this Saul and his hatred for Christians.

"At this moment," the Lord continued, "he is praying, having had a vision of a man called Ananias coming in and laying hands on him to give him back his sight."

"Lord, are you sure you have the right Ananias? I personally know at least ten other men by that name in Damascus, and there must be others," replied Ananias hopefully.

"Ananias, you are the one I want to go to Saul."

"But, Lord, several people have told me about this man and all the harm he has been doing to your saints in Jerusalem. He has only come here because he holds a warrant from the chief priests to arrest everybody who invokes your name," said Ananias in one last-ditch effort to wriggle out of danger.

"You must go all the same," God said, "because this man is my chosen instrument to bring my name before pagans and pagan kings and before the people of Israel. I myself will show him how much he himself must suffer for my name."

To his great credit, Ananias's questions were only temporary manifestations of a healthy fear and not the visible edges of a deep-seated resistance. Without any further hesitation, Ananias obeyed God and went. When he came to Judas's house on Straight Street, he entered and found Saul. Ananias laid his hands upon him and said, "Brother Saul, I have been sent by the Lord Jesus, who appeared to you on your way here so that you may recover your sight and be filled with the Holy Spirit."

Luke writes that Saul instantly regained his sight, as though scales fell from his eyes. He was baptized on the spot and began to recover his strength after eating a little food. Thus was Saul launched on his mission of great historical importance. And a little-known Christian named Ananias played a big part in the event because he was in the habit of doing what the Lord told him to do. He obeyed. (Based on Acts 9:10-19 / JB.)

Jesus taught that we would bear fruit if we obeyed his commandments, so obedience is a condition of our fruitfulness. "By this my Father is glorified, that you bear much fruit, and so prove to be my disciples. As the Father has loved me, so have I loved you; abide in my love. If you keep my commandments, you will abide in my love, just as I have kept my Father's commandments and abide in his love" (John 15:8-10 / RSV). As Jesus' disciples we bear fruit in two senses. As the fruit of obedience in our own lives we take on the character traits of Jesus. We grow in the fruit of the Spirit. We also bear fruit in the lives of others by drawing them to the Lord and bringing them into his Church. Adding people to the kingdom is the fruit of evangelization.

Ananias is an example of fruitfulness in both senses. When he obeyed the Lord, boldness replaced his fear and he became a little more like his Master. As we have seen, his obedience was circumstantially important in the conversion of Saul. The fruit of Ananias's obedience pyramids through history, for by participating in bringing Saul to the Lord, he has a share in Saul's far-reaching evangelism.

LOVE ONE ANOTHER

Jesus left no doubt about the measure for our obedience. The one commandment he insisted on subsumed all the others. "This is my commandment: / love one another, / as I have loved you. / A man can have no greater love / than to lay down his life for his friends" (John 15:12-13 / JB). Jesus' expectation was plain, simple, and hard. His disciples were to be marked by love. Practically speaking, no matter what happens we are to respond according to the standard of love. There's no easy way out of that command, for it covers every situation, penetrates to every nook and cranny of our lives.

Jesus was setting a higher standard than merely affirming the Ten Commandments, which forbid behavior that damages our neighbor — you shall not kill, you shall not commit adultery, you shall not bear false witness, you shall not covet. Jesus' command encompasses all of these and demands more. Obeying Jesus involves more than ruling out harming others; it means putting ourselves freely at their disposal. Paul says it succinctly: "Bear one another's burdens, and so fulfil the law of Christ" (Galatians 6:2 / RSV).

When Jesus commanded us to love others, he was taking aim at our flesh, the dead weight of self-indulgence that drags us away from obeying him. He wanted to diffuse our self-reliant urge to say "No, I won't! I don't want to!" The inertia of our flesh is so great that without a move of grace we aren't able to fulfill the command. That's the whole point. We cannot obey Jesus unless we turn to the Holy Spirit for help.

Our flesh is vindictive, mean, stingy, unreliable, and lustful. Love requires mercy, kindness, generosity, faithfulness, and self-control. These qualities describe mutually exclusive patterns of behavior. Our flesh has us moving one way and the Lord wants us to turn around and go in the opposite direction. Paul teaches that the commandment regarding love can prevent our drift into self-indulgence and that only by yielding to the Spirit can we obey it:

"For you were called to freedom, brethren; only do not use your freedom as an opportunity for the flesh, but through love be servants of one another. For the whole law is fulfilled in one word, 'You shall love your neighbor as yourself.' But if you bite and devour one another take heed that you are not consumed by one another.

"But I say, walk by the Spirit, and do not gratify the desires of the flesh" (Galatians 4:13-16 / RSV).

So our obedience helps make us replicas of Jesus. When we obey the love commandment we must engage the power of the Spirit and apply it to our self-indulgence, transforming it.

CARL'S STORY

I began my career as a history professor at Grand Valley State Colleges, a cluster of schools near Grand Rapids, Michigan. Early in my tenure there, I decided I would be open about my relationship with the Lord without being pushy. If anyone gave me an opening, I would speak up, and in seven years there were many opportunities.

There was one memorable occasion on which I did not want to keep my resolve. It was the first day of school of a fall semester, and as I walked into my classroom, I noticed a young man sitting in the front row. As I began to call the roll, I sensed the Lord drawing my attention to this person, whom I will refer to as Carl. In the next few minutes I was horrified by what the Lord was clearly prompting me to do. I was sure he wanted me to approach Carl and say: "Carl, the Lord Jesus has urged me to tell you that he loves you and wants you to come to know him."

I said to myself, "Lord, do you realize how unprofessional that would be? College teachers just don't go up to their students and say things like that!"

Silence.

"I can't just go up to him and tell him," I continued my soliloquy. "Besides I'm not really sure it's you. If you want me to speak to Carl, you're going to have to make it clear somehow."

Silence. But I knew I wasn't off the hook. The original thought persisted.

Early in the afternoon the next day there was a knock at my office door. In walked Carl, handed me a pink card, and announced, "Professor Ghezzi, I have just been assigned to you as an advisee and I came to talk." You would think that this development would have been enough to persuade me to obey, but I was still reticent. It was only on our third visit later that month that I finally gathered the courage to tell him.

"Carl," I began, clearing my throat, "I don't know how this is going to strike you, but there is something I have been wanting to say to you."

"Yes, sir?" said Carl.

"Well, when I first saw you, I had a sense in my thoughts . . . I thought I heard the Lord Jesus urge me to tell you that he loves you and wants you to come to know him." I had blurted it out and was waiting for Carl's reaction.

"I needed to hear that," he said. "You should have told me sooner." He was simply stating a fact, not trying to make me feel guilty, though I did. I apologized.

So began my friendship with Carl. In the next few months he came to my office often and visited several times with my family. I learned that Carl had a nominally Christian upbringing, that he really knew little about the Lord or Christianity. He was eager to learn and asked many questions. One night I explained in detail what it meant to enter into a personal relationship with Jesus. Before I knew what was happening, he knelt down in the middle of our living room, and prayed, inviting Jesus into his life.

Then things began to happen. I knew early in our friendship that Carl was living with his girlfriend (let's call her Sandra), but I deliberately ignored it. I was sure that was something the Lord would handle, and soon after Carl turned to him, he did. The next week Carl dropped into my office and said somewhat casually, "I have been thinking that the Lord wants me to stop living with Sandra. What do you think about that?" he asked.

"I think you're probably right," I said. I don't know any details, but he must have handled it well. The young couple set their relationship right and continued to see each other.

For the next two years I met with Carl regularly, studying the Bible with him and teaching him about the Christian life. He began to go to church with Sandra and received his baptism there. Week by week I watched him mature as a Christian. He grew in love of God; he began to orient his life around God's concerns; he prayed regularly; he studied the Bible and applied it to his life; he was eager to serve others; he got involved in his church. After Carl graduated, he married Sandra. Together for the last fifteen years they have faithfully served the Lord and are raising their family to follow him too.

Carl's story is about obedience and fruitfulness. Once Carl had a personal relationship with Jesus, he wanted to obey him. When he saw something in his conduct that conflicted with a commandment, he changed, as he did when he and Sandra stopped living together. Carl was in earnest, not merely toeing the line. He conformed his life to Christ's standard and he did a good job of it. I had the joyful privilege of watching as this young man put off his self-indulgence and put on the character of Christ.

I also learned about obedience and fruitfulness. From that time I became more courageous, emboldened to do whatever the Lord wanted me to. And I saw how my simple obedience, even though it came late, opened a boulevard for the Lord in Carl's and Sandra's lives, a road they are still walking together many years later.

At the wedding at Cana, Mary spoke to Jesus about the dwindling wine supply. She expected he would do something to spare the bride and groom any embarrassment. Knowing that Jesus would not refuse her, Mary said to the servants, "Do whatever he tells you" (John 2:6). Jesus told the servants to fill six large stone jars with water, draw some out, and take the water to the steward, who, upon tasting it, was astonished. The Lord had turned ordinary water into excellent wine, a miracle he worked out of love for his mother.

When we do whatever the Lord tells us, miracles still occur. Our obedience is a channel for our transformation in Christ, and it may be a key to new life for someone who does not know the Lord.

Imitating Christ 16

Several times a year, Sunday supplements feature lists of heroes that teenagers look up to, or in some cases go so far as to worship. Male and female rock stars and box-office leaders dominate these polls. TV idols, athletes, and an occasional astronaut or presidential hopeful round them out. Almost always nine of ten are unworthy of this recognition, which they win only because of their media exposure. I refrain from recording any names from current lists, because they change so rapidly that merely mentioning them would mar this book by dating it.

The desire for heroes runs so deep in us that when we are not given wholesome examples, we latch on to whoever happens to be on the rise. This accounts for the hero worship of these popular stars and other anti-heroes, which is a healthy human tendency gone berserk.

Among my earliest heroes were several outstanding high-school and college teachers. I admired them because they were intelligent, purposeful, and were able to make sense out of things. They seemed to have confronted and mastered life's complexities. They represented something I valued, I hungered for, and did not yet have.

Heroes are important to us because they embody our ideals. These are goals we strive for but have not reached. Ideals are targets we set our aim on, such as success, power, pleasure, wealth, service, generosity, or love of God. They always exist outside of ourselves and speak enticingly to the deep longings of our heart. As an adolescent I longed for purpose and mastery of knowledge, and I admired and honored people who represented these values.

As a child I had another group of heroes. In grade school, we were given a thick red book entitled *Little Pictorial Lives of the Saints*, which told the stories of holy men and women, one for each day of the year. For several years I read an item from it every school day. The total dedication to God and the selflessness of these people attracted me. I wanted to be like them. I shudder at the thought that God may have been listening to me when I prayed for a martyrdom like that of those Scandinavian Christians who were made to stand naked on a frozen lake because they refused to renounce Christ. And just to play it safe, I've moved to Florida.

THE PRINCIPLE OF IMITATION

Heroes evoke an intensely personal response from us. We aspire to be like them in every way, so we imitate them in detail. We copy their distinctive behavior and their speech. We may dress like them, mimic their idiosyncrasies, and so on.

Imitation is standard operating equipment in human beings, a part of our normal learning process. Along with instruction, experimentation, observation, and other principles, imitation is a strong, natural tool we use to shape our character. It is one of the ways we learn how to conduct ourselves as mature men and women.

Imitation often works unconsciously, as was observed above in Chapter 13, *The Apple Does Not Fall Far from the Tree.* Our concern there was with the Lord's part in our Christian formation, acknowledging that we become significantly more like Jesus simply by spending time praying in his presence. That personal transformation comes not by imitation but by the operation of grace, the intervention of the Holy Spirit.

Imitation also works deliberately. When we identify someone we admire, we may decide to become like that person. This principle is a tool that we can use in forming the character of our children, if we direct them to excellent models. Undirected, imitation works as if by automatic pilot, resulting in aberrations such as antihero worship. The principle, however, is not limited to children. We do it throughout our lives.

IMITATING CHRISTIANS

Christianity has always used the principle of imitation in the formation of believers. One reason God became man in Christ was to show us how to live as his sons and daughters. Jesus is the Son of God, made in his image and likeness. Scripture presents him as the firstborn from the dead, a second Adam who has founded a new race of men and women (Colossians 1:15-20). He alone reveals the Father to us (John 14:9), and he is the model of life for all who choose to be his disciples. Jesus said, "If anyone wants to be a follower of mine, let him renounce himself and take up his cross and follow me" (Matthew 16:24 / JB). Christians are supposed to pattern their lives on the Father and the Son. Paul wrote, "Therefore be imitators of God, as beloved children. And walk in love, as Christ loved us and gave himself up for us, a fragrant offering and sacrifice to God" (Ephesians 5:1-2 / RSV).

The early Christians developed a way of life that they taught throughout the Church. Some of this practical tradition has been preserved in the New Testament, especially in Paul's letters. (See, for example, Ephesians 4:17—6:24.) The Christian teachers, however, did not simply talk about how to live. They gave the Church living examples. They knew that instruction that was "all tell and no show" would be ineffective.

Paul often exhorted communities to follow his example. He told the Corinthians, "Be imitators of me, as I am of Christ" (1 Corinthians 11:1 / RSV). To the Christians at Thessalonica he wrote, "You observed the sort of life we lived when we were with you, which was for your instruction, and you were led to become imitators of us, and of the Lord" (1 Thessalonians 1:5-6 / JB).

Paul sent Timothy to Corinth and left Titus in Crete as exemplars of the Christian faith. "That is why I beg you to copy me and why I have sent you Timothy, . . . he will remind you of the way that I live in Christ, as I teach it everywhere in all the churches" (1 Corinthians 4:17 / JB; see also Titus 2:7).

Christians were not only to imitate their leaders, but they were also to look to others who were growing up in Christ. Paul said, "Brethren, join in imitating me, and mark those who so live as you have an example in

140

us" (Philippians 3:17 / RSV). Paul even recommended whole communities for imitation (1 Thessalonians 1:7).

READ, MEDITATE, IMITATE

Harry S. Truman was a voracious reader of biographies. Shelves stuffed full of life stories lined many walls of his home in Independence, Missouri. He devoured these books because he wanted to learn how others handled power with integrity. While I do not hold up Truman as a paragon of Christian virtue — although I think he was a good man — I recommend we copy his habit of studying others. Today we can still model our lives on Jesus, on Paul, and other early Christians by reading Scripture and meditating on it.

For example, let me tell you how reflecting on a Gospel passage affected my character. On one Sabbath day, a group of Pharisees watched as Jesus cured a man with a withered hand (Mark 3:1-6). The scene in the synagogue rippled with tension, as the Lord asked them if it was lawful to do good on the Sabbath. Mark tells us that Jesus "looked around at them with anger, grieved at their hardness of heart," and cured the man (Mark 3:5 / RSV).

As I reflected on Jesus' conduct here, I was impressed by his use of anger, which he kept under control, and I was startled by his healing while angry. The Lord's behavior persuaded me that Christians could be good and angry, so long as they controlled such anger. I began to see that if I was angry for a good reason that did not mean I had to wait to do the right things. Seeing Jesus use anger wisely moved me to express my anger with more deliberateness and restraint.

141

We should read Scripture expecting it to startle us with life-changing truths such as this. However, we should not confine our reading to the Bible. We should read widely in books and articles about Jesus and Christians who are worthy of our imitation. Many books of this kind have influenced me, but I will mention only one.

I have read and reread *Catherine of Aragón* by Garrett Mattingly. Catherine was the first wife of King Henry VIII, the one Henry decided to set aside, hoping Anne Boleyn could bear him a son. Catherine was a woman of strong Christian character. When the king wanted her to say that their marriage had not been consummated, she refused to lie, a decision which brought her much personal suffering. Letting Henry have his way without resistance would have been the easy way, but she chose the way of integrity instead. Her unflinching loyalty to God had a significant impact on the course of history, which is too complex to report here. I am sure some Church history buffs will track it down in Mattingly's book. For me, Catherine of Aragón will always be a model of standing up for the truth, no matter the personal consequences.

When we surround ourselves with excellent Christians like Catherine, we prepare ourselves to become more like Jesus.

IMITATION BY OBSERVATION

While we will find help in reading and meditating about model Christians, most of us will be affected more by living examples. For example, I have made it a practice of identifying young men and women, several years older than my children, who can serve them as models of good Christian qualities. Children find it easier to imitate people close to them in age than to follow their dad's instructions.

My oldest son, John, prayed with me every weekday morning during his high-school years. During that time two young men, both strong Christians, lived in our home. When John noticed that the three of us prayed each morning, he decided to join us. Those prayer times were not always especially deep — sometimes we were sleepy and sang off key — but they had a profound impact on my son's character. His habits of prayer are marked by what he learned there.

So we can enhance our efforts at spiritual growth by patterning our lives on exemplary Christians. Throughout our marriage, my wife, Mary Lou, and I have tried to become more like Christ by imitating good Christian friends. For example, we learned how to be generous from several remarkable Christians in our college environments. There was the poor family whose members always seemed to have something extra to give families in greater need, although they had very little themselves. There were the men and women, both teachers and students, who always had time to give counsel or aid to others, at great personal cost.

Mary Lou and I were so deeply influenced that we decided to imitate them. We began our married life with an excess of generosity that alarmed our parents. For example, we gave away all of our duplicate wedding gifts rather than exchange them. We donated a large chunk of our money gifts to our favorite outreach-to-the-poor program. Over the years the Holy Spirit trimmed us back a little and kept us on track. I think we learned real generosity, and imitation was the teacher.

When you imitate Christ, you don't get imitations. You get the real thing.

Walk by the Spirit 17

Have I persuaded you that your becoming more like Christ depends more on God's action than on yours? I hope I have, because it is the cardinal principle of spiritual growth. Without God's grace, no matter how hard you work, you cannot make yourself into a replica of Jesus.

It's not the case, however, that the less we do spiritually, the more we grow. Jesus did not teach us to be passive objects waiting in holy idleness for God to work in us. Just the opposite. The plain message of Scripture is that we must aggressively pursue our growth to Christian maturity. When the Bible talks about our part in the process, it uses action images:

• "Walk by the Spirit, and do not gratify the desires of the flesh" (Galatians 5:16 / RSV).

• "If we live by the Spirit, let us also walk by the Spirit" (Galatians 5:25 / RSV).

• "Put on then . . . compassion, kindness, lowliness, meekness, and patience" (Colossians 3:12 / RSV).

• "Let us also lay aside every weight, and sin which clings so closely, and let us run with perseverance the race that is set before us" (Hebrews 12:1 / RSV).

Our spiritual growth is the product of two energies working together, God's and ours, the first vast and the other small. Imagine linking the power of the greatest nuclear reactor with that of the tiniest combustion engine and setting both for the highest possible output. However puny it might seem in comparison to the reactor, from the little engine's perspective it is making a maximum contribution to the effort. It is giving all it has. That's a good way to look at our part in our Christian growth. We must work so hard that it can seem to us that we are doing it all ourselves, though we dare not become convinced of it.

Peter opens his second letter with a declaration of our role in cooperating with God's grace. He said that God's giving us a share in his divine nature is the reason we must do our utmost to acquire the fruit of the Spirit: "His divine power has granted to us all things that pertain to life and godliness, . . . by which he has granted to us his precious and very great promises, that through these you may . . . become partakers of the divine nature. For this very reason make every effort to supplement your faith with virtue, and virtue with knowledge, and knowledge with self-control, and self-control with steadfastness, and steadfastness with godliness, and godliness with brotherly affection, and brotherly affection with love" (2 Peter 1:3-7 / RSV). This passage sums up the connection between God's initiative and our response. If either one is missing, our growth to Christian maturity is not possible.

A DECISIVE BLOW

We do the hardest work for our Christian growth right in the thick of our daily struggles. Have you ever felt as though there were a war going on inside you?

Well, there is. Paul says that "the desires of the flesh are against the Spirit, and the desires of the Spirit are against the flesh; for these are opposed to each other, to prevent you from doing what you would" (Galatians 5:17 / RSV). The life of the Spirit in us runs smack into the inclinations of our flesh, the self-indulgence that is the residue of our old fallen natures. Our evil inclinations churn in us like a perpetual-motion machine that generates momentum toward sinful behavior. When evil desires are propelling us, it takes a decisive intervention to stop us.

In *Let the Fire Fall*, Michael Scanlan, the president of The Franciscan University of Steubenville, told how he once had to act forcibly against an evil desire: "On Good Friday evening I was driving home through one of the entertainment districts of Fort Lauderdale when I suddenly found myself in the grip of a nearly uncontrollable urge to park the car and sample some of the pleasures that surrounded me. I was mesmerized by the bright neon lights, enchanted by the sights and sounds of decadence. . . . It was the most powerful temptation I ever experienced. Only the most brutal act of the will kept me driving the car straight down the road until I got home."[23]

Our self-indulgent desires paint an alluring picture of evil. When we find ourselves wanting to do something wicked, we must say a definite no before we reach a point of no return. The Bible uses strong words like "crucify" and "kill" to describe the necessary action. Paul says we cannot even belong to Christ unless we "crucify all self-indulgent passions and desires" (Galatians 5:24 / JB). He also said, "You must kill everything

147

in you that belongs only to earthly life: fornication, impurity, guilty passion, evil desires and especially greed, which is the same thing as worshipping a false god" (Colossians 3:5 / JB). When Jesus said that the violent are taking the kingdom of heaven by storm (Matthew 11:12), I think one thing he had in mind was the violence we must use to refuse evil desires.

Saying no to temptation is hard, but grace is always there to help us. Have you noticed when you are circling in on some sinful behavior, that somewhere on the verge of acting you could have stopped; that there was a point along the path when you had just enough strength to refuse to go on? You should recognize that point as the moment the Holy Spirit is there prompting you to strike a decisive blow against self-indulgence.

LAUREL'S STORY

The trouble is, however, that we don't like to kill our evil passions. We prefer half-hearted measures to crucifying our flesh because we want to keep our options open. We are like the cartoon character Frank who confides to his friend Ernest: "I'm willing to flee temptation — if I can leave a forwarding address." Instead of saying no to temptation, we say "not right now," implying "maybe later."

Consider Laurel, for example. Laurel Gibson is a young Christian businesswoman who had a compulsive drinking problem. She says of her condition, "I seemed always to hear a little voice inside me that cried, 'More, more!' I had an inner compulsion to finish everything in the bottle, everything in my glass, even everything in everyone else's glass."[24]

148

Laurel could admit that she had a serious problem, especially on mornings after, but the thought of giving up drinking altogether was inconceivable — even repulsive — to her. When Doug, a business contact, decided he had to quit drinking, she affirmed her conviction that moderation was the only route for her. Total abstinence was completely out of the question.

However, on one morning when Laurel was suffering from the previous night's immoderation, God and events conspired to change her mind. She was unloading on Eileen, her roommate, who did not buy the theory that Laurel could opt for drinking in moderation. Then they spoke about Doug.

"Well," Laurel said, "I understand Doug used to drink quite a bit — like me, I guess. And he felt it was getting a hold on him, so he gave it up. I just can't see why he felt he had to do that."

"Why don't you ask him about it?" Eileen asked.

"Oh, Doug lives hundreds of miles away. And besides, when we do talk on the phone, we talk about business. A conversation about my drinking would change our relationship." Laurel was building up her defenses, because she expected a personal talk about her problem would be humiliating.

"I think you ought to ask him anyway. He could probably share some insights God has given him."

"Maybe," said Laurel, as she decided not to call him.

Moments later the phone rang. Eileen answered. "You won't believe it," she said. "It's your friend Doug calling long distance. Now go ahead and ask him!"

Perplexed, Laurel picked up the phone and said, "Hello?"

"Hi, Laurel, how are you doing?" answered Doug in a friendly voice.

"That depends. How much time do you have?"

"Oh, I've got time," he replied.

So Laurel confided in Doug, speaking openly about her hangover, her drinking problem, and her reaction to his decision to give up drinking. "Why on earth," she asked, "don't you try a more moderate approach?"

Before he explained, Doug told Laurel that as he was showering that morning he sensed God urging him to call her. "I heard God's voice as clearly as I've heard it only once before in my life. He said: 'Call Laurel Gibson.' I had no idea what it was about. I assumed it was about work."

In the next few minutes Doug shared his thoughts and experiences revolving around his own compulsive drinking, which was remarkably similar to Laurel's habit. "I realized," Doug explained, "after years of attempting moderation that I didn't really want just a little alcohol. I wanted *a lot* of alcohol. And that's where God drew the line for me. I wasn't able to use it; I had to abuse it. Given the opportunity, I still would. That's why I had to quit — completely. No half measures. It was all or nothing.

"You know, Laurel," he continued, "with something like giving up alcohol — or anything very hard — I think God has a special time for everyone. . . . I wonder if, right now, God isn't saying to you, 'Laurel, if you're willing to lay this thing down, I will pour out my grace on you so abundantly that it will even be easy for you to quit drinking.' "

God's presence in that conversation touched Laurel

deeply. Later she wrote, "Somehow Doug's words were becoming God's living word to me at that moment. I could hear his love in every syllable, and everything in me suddenly wanted to respond."

That morning, before going to work, Laurel decided to quit drinking. She says a pressure was released, and she was no longer consumed with the desire for an alcohol high or with planning opportunities to drink. Once she decided to strike a decisive blow — to kill her passion — the obsession left, a victory won by the combination of God's grace with the act of her will. In the years since that decisive morning, all has not been easy. When friends refill their glasses at social gatherings, dinner engagements, and the like, Laurel must say no, acknowledging her weakness, denying her self, and relying on the power of the Holy Spirit.

Laurel's story is an illustration of what St. Paul means when he says we must walk by the Spirit. Each time Laurel seizes the grace to crucify her flesh and refuse a drink, she grows in self-control, which is a fruit of the Holy Spirit.

BY THE SPIRIT

Ever since childhood we have enjoyed the thrill of accomplishment. "I'll do it *myself*" is a motto we display across our lives, like perpetual two-year-olds. This aspiration to do things for ourselves made sense when it was a matter of learning to tie our own shoes. However, the tendency to handle things on our own can be a block to our Christian growth.

Walking by the Spirit involves a shift that is both hard for us to see and hard to make. We must abandon the habit of acting on our own, and learn to act under the inspiration of the Holy Spirit. Problems spawned by the evil inclinations of our flesh drive the lesson home. How often have we met failure when we have attempted to tame the whirlwinds of greed or lust by sheer acts of our will? The futility of our own efforts, however, can be a blessing if it compels us to give up on doing it ourselves and to decide to do it in the Spirit.

Laurel, for example, tried to overcome her drinking problem by choosing moderation. It didn't work because her willpower was never strong enough to limit her compulsion. She was not able to deal with the problem until she made the shift from self-reliance to God-reliance. Now each time she feels the tug of desire toward drinking, she knows that if she lets the Holy Spirit work she has the strength to say no.

Walking in the Spirit does not mean disengaging our will. Our will still plays an important role, for it enforces our decision to engage the power of the Spirit in the problem area. Laurel must still exert enough willpower to refuse to accept the offer of a cocktail, but she doesn't need to have enough to conquer her alcoholism. Her attitude must be, "On my own, I'd end up drinking again, but with the Holy Spirit I can decline this drink."

I once counseled a young man who had a habit of masturbating and wanted to stop. I taught him about making the switch from trying to overcome his lust on his own to engaging the power of the Spirit to do it. He says he was finally able to break his habit when he learned to confront the sexual temptation. "I discovered," he told me, "that when I felt driven to masturbate I could resist the desire by referring it to the

Holy Spirit. I would tell it, 'I'm not giving in to you and I'm not even going to try to deal with you. You'll have to speak to the Lord about your proposals; he's taking care of those matters for me now.' " He was smart enough to see that he had just enough willpower to diffuse his lust by consigning it to the Holy Spirit. Once he made the shift, he saw a problem that had tormented him for a decade cease within a short time.

RAISE YOUR SAILS

Several years ago my family and I spent our summer vacation at a friend's cottage on a lovely Michigan lake. We had the use of his small two-person sailboat. I had no experience at sailing but was eager to try. My first adventure ended in miserable failure. Following my friend's instructions, I managed to get the boat across the lake, about a quarter of a mile from the house, struggling all the way. Then to my great frustration I could not figure out how to get back. Nothing I tried worked. I sat for more than an hour with no success, so I dove in the water, pulled the boat to the shallows, and towed it along the shore to our beach.

A little later on, my friend took me out in the boat. He taught me how to manipulate the sail to catch the breeze. He showed me the technique of tacking, which allows you to sail into the wind by angling back and forth. With a little practice, I was zipping along, my frustration turned to fun.

Learning to walk by the Spirit is like learning to sail. We can struggle along by our own effort and not get very far at all. But if we learn to raise our sails and catch the gentle yet powerful breezes of the Spirit, we will find ourselves moving briskly along in our Christian growth. Our work, like raising a sail, prepares us for the action of the Holy Spirit. Like the wind filling the sails, he empowers us and moves us directly on our course.

Chapter Notes

1. C.S. Lewis, *The Screwtape Letters & Screwtape Proposes a Toast* (New York: The Macmillan Co., 1973), pp. 37-38.
2. Nick Cavnar, "Jim Elliot: Apostle to the Aucas," *New Covenant* (May, 1980), pp. 9-12. See Elisabeth Elliot, *Shadow of the Almighty* (San Francisco: Harper & Row, Publishers, 1979).
3. See E. Beyreuther, "Good, Beautiful, Kind," in Colin Brown, editor, *The New International Dictionary of New Testament Theology* (Grand Rapids, Mich.: Zondervan, 1976), II, pp. 98-107.
4. See Beyreuther, p. 105.
5. H-H. Esser, "Mercy, Compassion," in Brown, II, p. 106.
6. Joseph Lahey, "The Day I Stopped Feeling Ashamed," *The Guideposts Treasury of Love* (New York: Bantam, 1982), pp. 270-272.
7. *The Orlando Sentinel*, September 10, 1986.
8. *New Covenant* (December, 1981), p. 14.
9. Anne Sandberg, "Old Maid," *New Covenant* (September, 1978), pp. 31-33.
10. Beck, C. Brown, "Peace," in Brown, II, p. 778.
11. Corrie ten Boom, *The Hiding Place* (New York: Bantam), pp. 199-200.
12. Tom Bradley, "My Two Built-in Blessings," in *The Guideposts Treasury of Love* (New York: Bantam, 1982), pp. 3-7.

13. U. Falkenroth and C. Brown, "Patience, Steadfastness, Endurance," in Brown, II, p. 771.
14. Boniface Hanley tells Kolbe's story in *Ten Christians* (Notre Dame, Ind.: Ave Maria Press, 1979).
15. See A.C. Thiselton, "Truth," in Colin Brown, editor, *The New International Dictionary of New Testament Theology* (Grand Rapids, Mich.: Zondervan, 1977), III, p. 879.
16. J.R.R. Tolkien, *The Two Towers* (New York: Ballantine Books, 1965), pp. 310-311.
17. Thiselton, pp. 878; 883-884; 885-886.
18. H-H. Esser, "Humility, Meekness (*tapeinos*)," in Brown, II, p. 262.
19. Alex Haley told John Newton's story in *Reader's Digest* (October, 1986), pp. 138-142.
20. *The New Oxford Annotated Bible with the Apocrypha; Revised Standard Version* (New York: Oxford University Press, 1973, 1977), p. 315.
21. See Thomas Green, *When the Well Runs Dry* (Notre Dame, Ind.: Ave Maria Press, 1979).
22. Phil Tiews, "Proven by Fire," *New Covenant* (February, 1982), pp. 16-18.
23. Michael Scanlan, *Let the Fire Fall* (Ann Arbor, Mich.: Servant, 1986), p. 185.
24. Laurel told her story in *Christian Life* (September, 1986), pp. 30-34.